nextstep

VOLUME 1

Discipleship is a series of next steps.

The Evangelical Catholic

theWORD
among us ®
Press

Published by The Word Among Us Press
7115 Guilford Drive, Suite 100
Frederick, Maryland 21704

23 22 21 20 19   1 2 3 4 5

ISBN: 978-1-59325-074-4
eISBN: 978-1-59325-372-1

Nihil Obstat: Msgr. Michael Morgan, J.D., J.C.L.
            Censor Librorum
            October 7, 2019

Imprimatur: +Most Rev. Felipe J. Estevez, S.T.D.
            Diocese of St. Augustine
            October 7, 2019

Made and printed in the United States of America.

Library of Congress Control Number: 2019915077

CONTENTS

Introduction

I knew the destination so well, but I still got lost the first time I drove myself to my family's annual vacation spot. On that first attempt at making the trip on my own, I noticed rock outcrops I'd never seen before and knew it was time to stop and get out the map.

Maps are available for most destinations, but where's the map that shows us how to grow closer to God?

Welcome to Nextstep!

Nextstep seeks to guide Catholics into a closer relationship with Jesus and to help them know Jesus better, to hear his voice more clearly, and to radiate his love more effectively. With an accompanying online resource from The Evangelical Catholic (ecnextstep.com), Nextstep uses a multimedia combination of story, witness, and teaching to guide users through practical and lively formation in the mission and habits of Jesus Christ and his followers.

Currently, Nextstep has four parts:

- **Find Your True North** seeks to solidify belief and clarify the mutual yes between God and each one of us, made possible through Jesus Christ, that constitutes the foundation of faith.
- **Explore the Terrain** and **Hit Your Stride** proceed through basic formation in the central habits and attitudes Jesus modeled, and these levels invite all of Jesus' followers to take up these habits, that we may continually grow into the freedom he came to give us.
- **Become a Guide** moves into the territory of mission, as the Lord sends each of his followers to partner with him in the ongoing transformation of the world.

This book contains parts 1 and 2 (Find Your True North and Explore the Terrain).

Each of the four parts contains six topics (chapters). Each page is brief, digestible in one to five minutes. You may progress through the pages at your own pace, but we encourage you to allow your reading and viewing to aid you in further prayer and reflection. Pause to reflect on what you just read, jot a few notes in a journal, and take your thoughts and questions to prayer.

While a program like this one can't adequately represent the full life of discipleship to which Christ calls each of us, we hope and pray it gives users an enjoyable, balanced, practical, and inspiring resource to launch ongoing personal and communal growth. We also hope it will fuel increased passion and zeal for the Lord!

Use Nextstep on your own, or invite a friend or small group to journey with you. If you embark on this journey with others, safeguard some personal reading and prayer times at home. Then get together regularly with others to discuss your thoughts, prayers, and reflections prompted by Nextstep content.

"Come, let us go up to the mountain of the LORD!"
Isaiah 2:3

Authorship and Style

Unless otherwise noted, written portions of this Nextstep experience were authored by Andre Lesperance and Andrea Jackson from The Evangelical Catholic. The writing also features occasional stories and contributions from current and former EC staff members Clare Freeman, Emily Mansfield, Kendra McClelland, and James Carrano.

All of the stories are true, though some names and minor details of select stories have been changed in order to ensure the privacy of others. While the contents within a given part or chapter will fluctuate between authors, the overall project is one collaborative work.

Bible Citations

Unless otherwise noted, all Bible citations are from the Catholic Edition of the Revised Standard Version of the Bible.

PART 1

FIND YOUR TRUE NORTH: WHO GUIDES YOUR LIFE?

1

The Gap

The gap between what we desire and what we experience is real.

A Gap Exists.

We all experience it.

A profound gap exists in our lives and in our world.

No matter our religious background, ethnic heritage, socio-economic status, or location on the planet, we all know this tension from experience: there's a gap between what the world is and what we wish, hope, or believe it could be.

If we're honest, we likely feel the same tension deep within *ourselves*. On the one hand, I believe I am good and I have some things to offer this world. And yet, I wish, hope, or believe I could somehow become . . . better, happier, healthier, more peaceful, more loving, or more effective.

More.

Or less: less selfish, angry, anxious, busy, fearful, or doubtful.

The gap may be big or small, and it may change over time. We may interpret its significance differently and offer conflicting accounts of its causes and effects. But one thing remains undeniable: the gap between what we desire and what we experience is real.

At some level, everyone knows the gap.

- **Where do you most see or experience the gap in the world?**

- **Where do you experience the gap in yourself?**

We Cannot Conquer the Gap.

We humans have a singular (even impressive) ability to manipulate the gaps *in* and *around* us. We really can make *the* world or *our own* world or *someone's* world better or worse. It's an amazing power and responsibility.

Yet despite this power, we cannot eradicate the gap, though we do try!

In our efforts to confront the gap, we likely turn to one of two approaches.

We may try to squelch our desire for a "better world" or a "better life." We lower our expectations, numb our pain, distract ourselves, or simply look the other way.

This method of dealing with the gap doesn't work. Sooner or later, we remember that we're deeply dissatisfied with some aspects of ourselves, others, or our world.

Or, if we can't ignore or numb the gap, we strive frantically to make ourselves and/or others conform to our ideas about the way things "should be."

This approach doesn't work either, and it usually leaves behind a trail of new hurts and disappointments.

* * *

Try as we might to remove the gap—by deadening our painful awareness of it or by defeating it through perfectionism and coercion—the gap remains. The ultimate story of the gap lies far beyond human control and understanding.

- **Which of the two strategies do you use when confronted with the painful gaps in your life?** A little of both for different situations.
- **Do you tend to soften your desire for something better? Or ramp up your efforts to make something happen?**

Perhaps you're an expert at both. Many of us are.

The Gap: A Source of Bigger Questions

Eventually (perhaps after we've faced enough failed attempts at "gap removal" in our lives), we may start asking some pretty big questions about the gap. Whether directly or indirectly, consciously or subconsciously, our confusing and painful experiences of the gap lead us to wonder about the deepest questions that have always rolled around in human minds.

These ageless questions fall into some general categories.

- **The question of origins:**
  - Where did we come from?
  - How did we get here?

- **The question of destiny:**
  - Where are we headed?
  - Is there anything after death?

- **The question of pain and suffering:**
  - Why is there so much pain in this life?
  - Is there any purpose or good to be found in it, or in spite of it?
  - If God exists and is good, how can he allow such suffering?

- **The question of happiness:**
  - What is true happiness and how can I attain it?

- **The question of conscience:**
  - What is right, and how do I know?
  - Is there even a real right and wrong?

- **The question of purpose:**
  - What is the meaning or purpose of our existence?
  - Of my existence?
  - Does my life make some kind of impact or contribution?

Simple - does not mean easy

The essential human questions might be summed up in one word: **why?**

- **What experiences in your life have drawn (or plunged) you into the deeper questions?**

- **What questions about your life do you have right now?**

- **If you could ask God anything and receive an answer, what would you ask?** Will this sinful nature pass from me. Am I strong enough to accept that I can do hard things. Can I follow you

Religions and Philosophies Make Attempts to Explain the Gap.

fully Can I give you control.

As we've discussed, the gap between what *is* and what we believe *could or should be* lies behind the deepest questions of the human mind and heart.

These ultimate human questions find expression, as well as answers, in various religions, philosophies, and ways of life. Systems of belief and practice offer possible "diagnoses" and "cures" to "fix" the universal experience of the gap.

Let's paint with some broad, oversimplified brushstrokes:

Early peoples believed the gods' anger caused the gap. They appeased the gods through sacrifices and rituals in an attempt to bring peace and abundance to their communities and, even, as they saw it, the world.

Marxists suggest the gap stems from private property and greed, and have argued in favor of achieving some sort of universal equality through common ownership of resources.

Buddhists believe the gap arises from deception, from a desire for unreal notions of the self and the physical world. Their solution involves eliminating desire and transcending the self through meditation and mortification.

The rock-and-roll, sexual-revolution adherent (and this group represents a sort of philosophical school) explains the gap as arising from the oppressive rules of authority figures and institutions, which inhibit the ideal of limitless freedom. The solution, for these individuals, lies in rejecting authority and doing "what comes naturally."

These accounts represent extremely limited pictures of the intricacies of actual religions, philosophies, and lifestyles, but they help lead us to the real questions:

- **What does Catholicism have to say about the gap?**
  Jesus is the way, God is the answer.
- **What does Catholic Christianity claim as the origin, fundamental diagnosis, and ultimate solution for the gap?**
  God - nothing else we need the Lord. We need
  How would *you* attempt to answer these questions? *to humble ourselves.*

The Good News?

The rest of this "apprenticeship" will present the basic Christian understanding of the gap: its origin, fundamental diagnosis, and ultimate solution.

But first, a question to ponder.

In the face of the gap, Jesus preached and embodied the "gospel," which means "good news." Since then, the word "gospel" has become a code word to summarize the entire message of the Christian faith.

What is this good news?

What is this good news that . . .

- . . . emboldened early Christians to endure torture and death while offering forgiveness to persecutors and giving praise to God?
- . . . motivated Mother Teresa (and many others) to start organizations dedicated to the poorest of the poor?
- . . . has propelled missionaries all over the world, throughout the centuries and today, to leave the comforts of a homeland in order to share its message with strangers?
- . . . fuels the institution that gave rise to the concepts of education for all, the university, and hospitals and social services for the poor?
- . . . leads some to trade the prospect of a family for heroic service to the Church?
- . . . empowers others to commit unconditionally to spouses and children with the equally heroic love demanded by family life?
- . . . compels the generous and sacrificial sharing of time, talent, and treasure for the sake of every just cause?

- **How would you summarize the good news?**

  We are all children of God

In a Nutshell

Many, many ways exist to capture the core truths proclaimed as good news at the heart of the Catholic faith.

The *Catechism of the Catholic Church* provides a concise summary in its opening paragraph. As you read it here, allow it to prompt deeper reflection. The questions below can help.

God, infinitely perfect and blessed in himself, in a plan of sheer goodness freely created man to make him share in his own blessed life. For this reason, at every time and in every place, God draws close to man. He calls man to seek him, to know him, to love him with all his strength. He calls together all men, scattered and divided by sin, into the unity of his family, the Church. To accomplish this, when the fullness of time had come, God sent his Son as Redeemer and Savior. In his Son and through him, he invites men to become, in the Holy Spirit, his adopted children and thus heirs of his blessed life.[1]

- How does this summary of the good news account for the gap between what is and what could or should be? *point to where we should look. Wants a relationship with us.*
- What fundamental diagnosis and ultimate cure does the Church propose here? *We can't do it on our own. We need God*
- How does this paragraph give seeds of an answer to some of the questions of human searching: questions of origin, destiny, suffering, happiness, and purpose?

- **Are there any phrases that illuminate your own experience or prompt deeper questions for you?**

Five Truths about Ourselves

Have you ever gotten one of those toy animals or washcloths that come packed in a tiny capsule the size of a pill? When you soak it in water, it gradually unfolds to reveal a surprisingly large item. Only after soaking it do we see what the thing is. Before we soak it, the thing's design, beauty, and function sit hidden away.

The first paragraph of the *Catechism* is a bit like that animal to be soaked, as is the creed. The central truths of our faith sit tightly bound up in one small place. Their true beauty, truth, and goodness are there, though mostly hidden.

For the rest of part 1, we will soak this condensed pill of the good news to reveal its truth.

We will examine the good news through the lens of what it teaches us about God and ourselves. We will highlight five central claims about our identity that flow from this good news.

We are:

1. God's beloved,
2. broken by sin,
3. rescued by grace,
4. being transformed, and
5. free to respond.

Website -
- should take about a few weeks

· We have our own personal story

· Prayerfully reflect on our past.

· The idea to go to God with
  problems.

2

God's Beloved

Now do you know how much I love you?

If God Is Love

1 John 4:8 makes an extraordinary claim: "God is love."

Not just that God loves or that God loves a lot but that God *is* love.

What might this mean?

The *Catechism* explains, "God's very being is love. By sending his only Son and the Spirit of Love in the fullness of time, God has revealed his innermost secret: God himself is an eternal exchange of love, Father, Son and Holy Spirit, and he has destined us to share in that exchange" (221).

How might this truth answer some of those great human questions?

Here are a few possible implications, from the Christian tradition, to ponder:

- Love was first. Before the universe existed, there was love.
- Love will be last. Though much in this world will crumble and fall, love remains. Love is eternal.
- Love is the reason for our existence. We were loved into being.
- Love is the strongest possible force and the most real reality.
- ✳ Love wins. In whatever struggles and battles may lie ahead between love and whatever opposes love, love will gain the ultimate victory. *Am I the prize?*
- Love is personal. Love is infinitely and eternally exchanged between the Persons of the Trinity.
- We are granted the opportunity to share in this eternal, infinite, perfect love of God.

- **Which of these claims means the most to you right now?**
  Love wins. In whatever struggles
- **Can you think of other implications of the truth that "God is love" (1 John 4:8)?**
  Whoever does not love, does not know God. For God is love.

God Loves Me (So What?)

If you were to survey 100 Catholics and ask them to summarize the central message of Christianity in a few phrases or sentences, you might hear 99 of them use the word "love" somewhere in their answer. If Catholic religious education in the past 50 years has made anything stick in our minds, it might just be the idea that God loves us.

But does believing in a loving God really matter to us? Does it make a difference in our lives?

Andre

At times I have struggled, struggled greatly, painfully even, to know God's love in a personal and meaningful way. It can be easy to think of God's love as a distant concept, rather than as an actual loving relationship between persons.

If I'm honest, sometimes—even subconsciously—I imagine God's love more like that of a rock star who says, "I love all my fans" without really knowing any of them.

Or sometimes God's love seems like a different kind of star: a flaming ball of gas constantly emitting heat and light (love) somewhere far, far away. It's there, no question about it. I can even see it sometimes. But it always lies far off in the distance. It's not like the rays of the sun, which I can feel on my face, and which illuminate everything around me.

Such a general, distant "love" isn't much to write home about.

- How do you understand the phrase "God is love" (1 John 4:8)? *We can't truly know God unless we know and believe his love for us. How do I recipercate his love.*
- Do you ever struggle to know, feel, or believe in God's personal, intimate, and caring love for *you*?

self worth *Always, I know he loves me I just don't know why. because we are his sons and daughters his creations*

Our Hearts Can Doubt What Our Heads Believe.

Andre

One of the more illuminating times in my spiritual life arose through some of the most intense suffering I had yet undergone. In the midst of this disorienting pain, in which my self-understanding and my faith in God were twisted, stretched, and (so I thought) almost shattered, I came to realize something simple and profound: our hearts can doubt what our heads are convinced is true.

This realization opened for me the way to more discovery and freedom.

With my intellect, I believed fully in God's existence and in his care for me.

But my heart wasn't sure.

With my powers of *reason*, I agreed with all the brilliant minds who have articulated the Catholic faith with subtlety and grace. But my *heart* felt, and feared, the possibility that it could all be fake.

With my *mind*, I could look at all the ways God had guided and provided for me over the years. But my *heart* needed a real, immediate assurance that my heavenly Father saw me, knew me, and cared for me.

This need for reassurance affected my sense of self. In my head, I knew I offered something valuable to others. But my heart called this value into question, bringing debilitating pain.

"And you will know the truth, and the truth will make you free," said Jesus (John 8:32).

Indeed. But this type of knowing surely goes deeper than a cerebral "agreeing with." It must, somehow, reach to the depths of our hearts.

Once I started learning to let Jesus meet me, not just in my head-space of thoughts, reason, doctrines, and plans, but in my heart-space of longings, fears, hopes, doubts, and insecurities, I began to taste yet again—and even more deeply—the radical freedom of the children of God.

- Does your heart ever tend to doubt things your head thinks are true? If so, what kinds of things?

  Always - All kinds of things, Hard to explain but they are there.

Hearing God Say, "I Love You"

Andre

In the midst of my pain and suffering, I learned that I didn't merely need some well-intentioned friend or mentor reminding me that I'm loved by God. I needed a fresh encounter with the One who loves me. What I had always known and believed in my head (and taken for granted, feeling tempted to write it off as a trite, obvious truth for children's books), I needed to learn, to hear, to believe, to *experience* once again.

During this time of deeper searching, I encountered Fr. Ronald Rolheiser's discussion of a retreat he had attended. While the retreatants were hoping for some novel, sophisticated insights from the retreat master, what they received was something "stunningly simple and down-to-earth."

Rolheiser summarized the master's insight this way:

You must try to pray so that, in your prayer, you open yourself in such a way that sometime—perhaps not today, but
sometime—you are able to hear God say to you, "I love you!"
These words, addressed to you by God, are the most important words you will ever hear because, before you hear them,
nothing is ever completely right with you, but after you hear
them, something will be right in your life at a very deep level.[2]

- **What is your reaction to this simple—and quite bold—statement?** It seems so simple and yet I struggle everyday. We need to open ourself
- **Do any of the retreat master's words capture your own experiences?** I know it sounds easy and true enough, but still I struggle

We don't want to hear it.
We Are God's Beloved.

Though words will always fall far short of real experience,
they remain immensely important. And few words carry the
power and significance of "I love you." To hear these words
with the *ears of our hearts*, uttered from the God of the universe
uniquely to each of us . . . well, that is a grace of inestima-
ble worth.

We cannot force this event to happen. We cannot demand
that God speak in a certain way or time frame. Nor should
we grow discouraged or blame ourselves if we go for long
stretches of time without hearing God's voice. But let us not
be ashamed to admit that we *long to know* that God loves us
and cares for every detail of our lives.

Under the loving gaze of God, each of us is

- A beloved child,
- unique and unrepeatable,
- seen, known, and loved, and
- a possessor of an inherent dignity, goodness, and worth that no one can take away.

Perhaps parents have an especially privileged window into the kind of love the Father has for all his children. A man named James tells the story of his son's first moments of life. James and his wife Jess were at the hospital, elated and exhausted, their infant son in James' arms. James' own father had come to visit and stood beside James, studying his son and grandson. His eyes incandescent, James' father leaned over and whispered to James, "Now do you know how much I love you?"

Our Father in heaven will seize the right opportunity in each of our lives to ask the same question.

Waiting to Hear

Andre

My own time of trial and suffering came to an end rather gradually and anticlimactically. Eventually, my heart simply found *something*, found God's comfort. I *did* "hear," once again, God say how much he loves me. And Fr. Rolheiser's retreat director was right; once again, "something" has been made right in my life at a very deep level.

But that does not mean there will not be more seasons of waiting to hear of, to *experience*, that self-emptying, pure, and perfect love, a love beyond anything I have ever known in this world. In different ways and in various times throughout our lives, we all wait to hear him whisper to us, "Now do you know how much I love you?"

We *are* God's beloved.

- **How is this aspect of *the* good news good news to *you*?**

    Its already something I know I just need to feel it.

- **In what area of your life or in what recesses of your heart do you most need to hear this good news?**

    In all the recesses (self worth)(affrimations)

- **Can you ask the Lord to tell you this—in whatever way and time frame he knows will best serve you?**

    We can always ask. can we be patient enough to hear it? Are we strong enough?

Prayer Intentions -

· Connie - Gene's Family Dixic & my parents.

· Alene - for those that are scared of virus that they can find peace. Faith trust in God.

Kathy - Ava-meds makes her more anxious - werid funk.

Liz - Cady - internalize a lot
Help her to find peace

3

Broken by Sin

One thing is certain: we all contribute, in some way, not only to what is right and good in this world, but also to what is broken.

The Dividing Line

Andre

My daughter Madeline loves when I read her the children's books that bear her name. In those *Madeline* books, Miss Clavel, the teacher of the twelve girls at boarding school, often awakes in the middle of the night with a start, intuiting, "Something is not right!" She runs to the girls, and sure enough, something is quite wrong!

Of all the Catholic teachings, the doctrine of original sin is probably the easiest to build a case for. Just look around; it's pretty clear that "something is not right!" As we said earlier, the gap exists.

In the Christian tradition, "sin" is the broadest name we give this *something* that is *not right*. Sin causes many of the gaps in our lives and in our world. Sometimes it is our own sins causing gaps in our lives and in the lives of others. Sometimes the sins of other people do this for us. Our world is a complex web of darkness and light. One thing is certain: we all contribute, in some way, not only to what is right and good in this world, but also to what is broken. For "all have sinned and are deprived of the glory of God" (Romans 3:23, NABRE).

Humans are both deeply good and dangerously conflicted. None of us are exempt from this complexity. Indeed, "The line dividing good and evil cuts through the heart of every human being."[3] Honest people need look no further than their own lives for corroborating evidence.

- **What is one way you see the dividing line running through your heart?**

What Is Sin?

Sin is an offense against God, self, and others.

The *Catechism* explains further: Sin "is failure in genuine love for God and neighbor caused by a perverse attachment to certain goods. It wounds the nature of man and injures human solidarity" (1849).

Much is said here. Let us briefly expand upon three points.

First, sin is failure to love. To love means to will the good of the other. The greatest commandment, which Jesus said summed up and interpreted all the others, is to love God, neighbor, and self (we see this idea in Matthew 22:36-40).

Second, since all that God created is fundamentally good, it is *good* things we seek when we sin. But our pursuit is characterized by a perverse attachment. Food is good, but gluttony is perverse. Sexual love is good, but lust is a perversion. Like Adam and Eve clutching at the fruit that God did not give them as a gift, we twist ourselves and the goods we seek by seizing that which is not properly given as a gift.

Third, sin wounds our nature and our communion. While we were created to share in the loving communion of the Trinity, in harmony with all of creation, we experience a series of strained or broken communions in this life. Both our own sins and the sins of others contribute to at least four ruptured relationships:

- between us and God (spiritual),
- between us and others (social),
- between us and nature (ecological), and
- within us (physical, psychological).

- **Which of these strained or broken communions feels most pressing to you right now?**

Sin Is Idolatry.

"Idolatry" provides another word we might use to express the idea of a "perverse attachment to certain goods." In the Old Testament, idolatry usually took the form of worshipping other gods. But all people, whatever their historical or cultural/religious context, experience the temptation to put themselves, another person, or a certain good in the center of their lives—a place designed only for the one true God.

Identifying idolatry (sin) in our lives can be difficult. We rarely see how much weight we are giving certain fears, pursuits, and desires deep within us.

It can help to speak not just of sin in general but of particular sins. What are these sins that break the necessary communions in our world?

The ancient tradition enumerating seven deadly sins has long provided a remarkably consistent way to answer that question. We describe these sins as "deadly" because of their power to injure, and even to kill, relationships meant for communion and harmony.

THE DEADLY SIN OF	IS AN IDOLATRY OF
Pride	Self
Envy	Status or Possessions
Gluttony	Food or Drink
Lust	Sex or Relationship
Anger	Control or Justice
Greed	Security or Wealth
Sloth	Comfort

For each of these sins, we can also point to the certain good which they seize in an unhealthy way or degree.[4]

- **Does this deepen your understanding of sin?**

- **Is there one sin that is especially prevalent in your life right now?**

Sin and Wounds: A Vicious Cycle

Sin "wounds the nature of man and injures human solidarity" (*Catechism*, 1849).

All sins inflict wounds. They wound the one who commits them, they wound those directly wronged by the sins, and they wound the four relationships of communion we discussed a couple pages ago in "What Is Sin?" (namely, our relationships with God, others, nature, and ourselves).

While sin leads to wounds, wounds can also lead to sin. When we are hurting from wounds like abandonment, fear, confusion, rejection, powerlessness, shame, and hopelessness,[5] we often turn to sin (rather than God) as a false form of comfort. We may eat too much, drink too much, watch too much TV, overuse social media, escape into an erotic or emotional fantasy, or strive desperately to prove our worth through various praise-winning projects. Or we may dump our wounds on others by lashing out verbally at family members, becoming impatient with friends, or gossiping about coworkers.

False comforts can work to distract us from our pain or bring quick relief—for a time. But they do not heal our wounds.

They only numb the pain for a bit. Unhealed wounds, no matter how small at first, are prone to infection. They grow and spread. When this happens, we consume *larger* doses of our false comforts. A vicious cycle develops: our pain leads us to sin's doorstep, and sin only causes more pain in the long run.

We've all been wounded by the brokenness and sins of others. We've all been wounded by our own attempts to numb our pain through false comforts. It takes humility and God's grace to understand and admit that we are not exempt from this vicious cycle. It's a crucial step toward grasping the gospel, and toward healing and growth.

• **Where do you see elements of this vicious cycle in your life?**

Our Need for a Savior

It's never fun to identify the vicious cycle of sins and wounds in our own lives. It's also notoriously difficult to identify the cycle. Much of what is in our hearts or behind our thoughts and actions remains hidden from our sight. It's a grace just to admit this obscurity, as St. Paul does in Romans 7:15: "I do not understand my own actions."

The good news (and remember, our context for this topic *is* good news!) is that we don't need to fully see, understand, or diagnose our sins and wounds. The Lord will lead us in rooting out every weed in due time. But first, let us continually confess our need for a Savior. We cannot "fix" ourselves or our world on our own. We cannot heal our wounds, transform our pain, or heal others on our own.

This is profoundly good news! But only because of one unshakeable, all-important truth, which is the subject of the next module: we are *not* left alone. A Savior *has* been given. A divine Savior, a heavenly remedy, a rescuing God, who loves to heal, restore, and strengthen his weary children, exists! This saving God has come—in Jesus Christ and the Holy Spirit. He continues to come to us and is currently engaged in the work of our healing.

Jesus said, "Those who are well have no need of a physician, but those who are sick; I came not to call the righteous, but sinners" (Mark 2:17).

Can you call out to Jesus for some way you need his saving help? If so, you're in good company, and you're a good candidate for "getting" what Jesus is all about.

Truth and Lies

Emily

Throughout college, I struggled to trust and hope in God's love and mercy. A friend suggested that I write out lies that I believed about myself, about God, and about how God thought of me. She suggested writing something along the lines of "I reject the lie that . . ." and countering that lie with truth: "I affirm the truth that . . ."

I went before Jesus in Eucharistic Adoration and started to write out the lies that most discouraged me, that caused great sadness (for example, "I reject the lie that my sins are too great for God to forgive"). In searching for truth to replace these lies, the first responses coming to mind were worldly truths: that I deserved praise since I tried to "be good" or that I hadn't really sinned but could put blame on my circumstances.

Finally, I felt deeper truth starting to sink in, bringing a sense of peace. I needed to embrace my brokenness to allow the Father a chance to lovingly fill me with truth. Truthfully, I was broken, but God restored me in knowing myself as his beloved daughter. I had sinned, but God compassionately welcomed me into his arms. I couldn't earn God's love by any accomplishment, but he delighted in giving me good gifts and dispelling my fears. I was starting to learn that I can love even the parts of me that are broken because God wants to meet me exactly in those places.

4

Rescued by Grace

He's defeated every enemy.
He's opened the floodgates of grace.

A Remedy Exists!

Andre

My son gets bloody noses quite often, so I'm accustomed to removing bloodstains from clothing, carpet, pillowcases, and furniture. Every time I set out to clean a stain, the seemingly magical power of hydrogen peroxide amazes me. This incredible substance attacks an otherwise permanent bloodstain, fizzing and bubbling it away into nothingness! What looked like an intolerable mess (or crime scene) a few moments ago gets restored back to its original beauty, and only one substance in the world could make it happen.

As we recalled in the last chapter, there is an intolerable mess in our broken world. Beauty and goodness surround us too, no doubt, but there's no denying the prevalence of sin, wounds, confusion, and darkness in our world and in our lives. We live in a bloodstained world. And no amount of mere soap and water can clean it all up. No amount of human effort or intelligence is enough to close *the gap* and restore the beauty.

Some people just throw up their hands and accept the gap as "the way the world is" and nothing more. (We talked about this approach in chapter 1, discussing how some people choose to lower expectations, or look the other way, rather than confront the gap.) It's a bit of the attitude: "Hope for the best, enjoy the good, avoid the mess when you can, and hold on for dear life when you can't. And maybe help a few others along the way."

But as Christians, we believe there is something powerful enough to do the job. We believe there is a "substance" that can heal every wound, cleanse every stain, break every chain, and triumph over every darkness the world has ever known. We believe in grace.

What Is Grace?

So God's grace is the only remedy for all the world's brokenness.

But what is grace?

The analogy of a uniquely powerful substance for removing the stains of human folly might communicate something of how we understand grace, but it also falls quite short. Grace is not a mere thing or substance. It is not magic. Nor is it quantifiable.

Grace is not so much an "it" or a "what" as a "Who." Grace is God's gift of *his very self* to his creation.

In the words of the *Catechism*, grace is . . .

- "the *free and undeserved help* that God gives us" (*Catechism*, 1996),
- "a *participation in the life of God*" (*Catechism*, 1997), and
- "the gift of the Spirit who justifies and sanctifies us" (*Catechism*, 2003).

Grace is the gift of God's love poured out for us in big and small ways: from the ultimate gift of salvation to his quiet, ready response to our daily needs. Looking at it one way, grace is God himself walking with us through it all.

- **What moments, seasons, or events stand out in your life as the most memorable experiences of grace?**

- **Can you identify a small grace-filled moment from the last few days and give thanks?**

The Source of All Grace

While God has always aided those who seek him with a sincere heart, the floodgates of grace opened when God *himself* came into our world as a human and accomplished the definitive act of our salvation by his death and resurrection. It is the mystery of mysteries, the most unimaginable, shocking claim: the Creator of all, who is pure spirit and "dwells in unapproachable light" (1 Timothy 6:16) took on human flesh, lived as a character on our own broken stage, bearing the weight of the world's sin upon his own innocent self. He suffered and died under the weight of this sin, thereby entering into the ultimate consequence of humanity's rejection of God: "For the wages of sin is death" (Romans 6:23). Then, by rising from the dead, Jesus won the victory over all that could potentially separate people (and all of creation) from God, namely, sin, evil, and death itself!

This is the unfathomable mystery of redemption wrought by Jesus Christ. Perhaps we've heard these or similar words so many times we forget how marvelous, shocking, and deeply transformative these truths really are. Or perhaps we're a bit perplexed as to how our salvation "works." If so, we're in good company! Theologians have filled libraries trying to understand and explain the intricacies of just *how* Jesus accomplished our salvation, but all Christians (from simple individuals to the most brilliant scholars) agree *that* Jesus saved us by his life, death, and resurrection.

> He saved us, not because of deeds done by us in righteousness, but in virtue of his own mercy, by the washing of regeneration and renewal in the Holy Spirit, which he poured out upon us richly through Jesus Christ our Savior, so that we might be justified by his grace and become heirs in hope of eternal life. The saying is sure. (Titus 3:5-8)

> For the wages of sin is death, but the free gift of God is eternal life in Christ Jesus our Lord. (Romans 6:23)

In Jesus, God revealed himself like never before, defeated every enemy, opened the floodgates of grace into the world, and inaugurated God's kingdom on earth. Jesus Christ is the fountain of all grace.

Only Jesus?

It is not uncommon for some believers to struggle with the bold, exclusive claims about Jesus in Scripture and Tradition. They might worry, consciously or subconsciously, that belief in one faith or religious figure over others makes one arrogant or even prone to condemn others. So these believers may start to waver in their views about Jesus. Maybe Jesus didn't really say things like "Without me you can do nothing" (John 15:5, NABRE) and "No one comes to the Father except through me" (John 14:6, NIV).

But ultimately, these doubting paths are dead ends. If Jesus is not the one true God, then he is not worthy of our worship, and the Catholic/Christian tradition is dangerously misleading. It is a decisive choice.

Accepting the primacy of Jesus Christ does not force the conclusion that only Christians can be saved. Catholic theology is richly satisfying and appropriately humble on this delicate topic. "For by His incarnation the Son of God has united Himself in some fashion with every man."[6] "The fact that the followers of other religions can receive God's grace and be saved by Christ apart from the ordinary means he has established does not thereby cancel the call to faith and baptism which God wills for all people."[7] God's ways are never limited to our feeble understandings.

We believe exclusively in Jesus because he alone is God.

Scripture and Catholic Tradition mince no words about the uniqueness and primacy of Christ. Jesus Christ is Lord of lords, King of kings, true God and true man. He is the unique source, center, and ultimate meaning of all things (we see this idea in Colossians 1:15-20). He is the fullness of divine revelation; he is the divine Physician who alone possesses power to remedy every ill; he is love itself, mercy itself, truth itself, justice itself, and the essence of every good thing. Jesus Christ is "the image of the invisible God" (Colossians 1:15), "the way, and the truth, and the life" (John 14:6). And "at the name of Jesus every knee should bow" (Philippians 2:10).

Embracing the real Jesus does not make us arrogant and does not mean we condemn others. It aligns our minds with the greatest truth of our existence and calls us to be more like him who laid down his life for his enemies.

- **Do you find it easy or difficult to accept these bold truths about Jesus?**

- **What questions do they raise for you?**

What Is Salvation?

Jesus came to save us. But what does this mean? How are we to understand this good news, this offer of salvation that can seem so remote at times?

- Did Jesus come merely to punch our tickets to a future heavenly paradise?

- Did Jesus come to establish perfect peace on earth and rid the world of sin, divisions, and pain?

- Did Jesus come to tell us how to fix the world, and then did he sit back and wait for us to accomplish this fixing?

There are many false or partial gospels that may float around our communities. How are we to understand—and, more importantly, experience—the good news Jesus came to proclaim?

We cannot sufficiently answer this question here. It demands not simply a "right answer," but a life of seeking, following, loving, and learning from Jesus. We all must bring our deepest questions, hopes, and longings to Jesus, asking him to show us what his salvation means—for us and for the world. If the gospel is true (and it is), the Lord *himself* will lead us on a path of adventurous discovery and transformation!

That last word—"transformation"—is one key to understanding the salvation that Jesus brings. This is the subject of our next chapter.

5

Being Transformed

It's not about being a good kid or a nice guy. It's about being like Jesus.

I Once Was Blind.

Andre

A few years ago, I had a roommate named Tony, who became a close friend. Tony is blind. Mostly blind, actually. Out of one corner of one eye, Tony can see a tiny bit of light. Tony reads Braille and walks with a white cane, and he spent over a decade unable to see any light whatsoever. Through surgery, doctors repaired one small section of Tony's right eye, allowing him to see that sliver of light. If Tony holds a book close to his eye, with the help of a magnifying glass, he can just make out some letters and read one word at a time.

Most of us probably can't imagine the difficulties of such a life. To only see a hint of light seems like a severe captivity. But to Tony, this little bit of light is infinitely more than the total darkness he has endured for all these years. He now notices when the sun comes out from behind a dark cloud. He can see the people he loves, even if they look like fuzzy shadows. To Tony, this recovery of imperfect sight is nothing less than a life-changing blessing, a (partial) transformation for which he is immeasurably grateful.

Surely, Tony wishes he could see more. Surely, he looks forward to that day when, in the resurrection of the body, he will see perfectly. He continues to struggle with physical blindness. But Tony takes very literally the lyrics from a timeless hymn: "I once . . . was blind, but now I see."

On a spiritual plane, I think there's something in Tony's story that is true of all of us baptized Christians.

The Doctor Is In.

Tony's physical situation can remind us of our spiritual situation, as well as that of the world at large: We don't "see" fully either. We're not yet fully healed of all our wounds and sins. We don't understand truth fully; our reasoning can be distorted. The brokenness of creation still holds considerable sway in the universe and in each of our lives. But just as in Tony's life, darkness is not all there is to our story. Light *has* broken through; healing *has* begun!

The light is Jesus Christ. "In him is no darkness" (1 John 1:5). Even more, the doctor is in! Jesus is the divine Physician who has already begun his surgery to open the eyes of our hearts to the light of God's kingdom (see Luke 5:31-32).

Like Tony, we don't take in all of this kingdom light at once. "For now we see in a mirror dimly" (1 Corinthians 13:12). But if we remain with him, with Jesus, we shall one day see God "face to face" (13:12). The fullness of God's kingdom is not here yet, but the kingdom broke into our world when the King made his visit to earth. Ever since then, Baptism has become our entry into this kingdom of God. The Church is the society of people eagerly undergoing (and *participating* in) a transformation whose beauty and immensity we scarcely even fathom.

Immeasurably More

Salvation is a process: a long, grace-filled journey of transformation in Christ. It is difficult to speak of this journey in a way that even comes close to doing justice to the unfathomable promises of God. Consider just a few Scriptural promises, which speak both of the journey and of the final destination.

- "He will wipe away every tear from their eyes, and death shall be no more, neither shall there be mourning nor crying nor pain any more, for the former things have passed away" (Revelation 21:4).
- "[T]he sufferings of this present time are *not worth comparing* with the glory that is to be revealed to us" (Romans 8:18, emphasis added).
- "[For he] is able to do *immeasurably more than all we ask or imagine*," according to his power that is at work within us (Ephesians 3:20, NIV, emphasis added).

- "[W]e all . . . are being transformed into his image with ever-increasing glory" (2 Corinthians 3:18, NIV).
- "His divine power has granted to us all things that pertain to life and godliness, through the knowledge of him who called us to his own glory and excellence, by which he has granted to us his precious and very great promises, that through these you may escape from the corruption that is in the world because of passion, and become partakers of the divine nature" (2 Peter 1:3-4).
- "[W]e shall be like him" (1 John 3:2).

• **What do you think such promises mean?**

• **Which of the promises on this page speaks to you the most?**

• **How does your heart react to these promises?**

Mr. Nice Guy

"He has granted to us his precious and very great promises, that through these you may . . . become partakers of the divine nature" (2 Peter 1:4).

What does it mean to be "partakers of the divine nature"?

For starters, it means a whole lot more than being a good person.

A friend told me recently how she was always a "good kid." You know the type. Stayed out of trouble, played nice with others, did well in school. According to her, it never even crossed her mind to sneak out at night or skip class. Her dad jokes that raising her only resulted in one of his gray hairs; her brother gave him the rest!

Most people are more or less good kids and nice guys. We figure, "Hey, I'm not going around killing people, and I don't cheat on my taxes; that's got to count for something."

What does it "count for"? Is being a good kid or a nice guy what Jesus expects of us?

The Church teaches that by virtue of our baptism, all Christians are called to holiness. *Holiness.* The deepness and richness and strength of *holiness* outstrip the good kid and nice guy qualities by miles. In Baptism, we "put on the Lord Jesus Christ," "cast[ing] off the works of darkness and put[ting] on the armor of light" (Romans 13:14, 12). St. Paul uses these clothing metaphors to signify a fundamental change in identity. When we "put on the Lord Jesus Christ," we take on Jesus' likeness and character. We toss out our old clothes and are made over into a new person, another Christ.

Holiness is not about being a good kid or a nice guy. It's about being like **Jesus.**

Becoming Jesus

"Becoming like Jesus" is a great description of holiness, but there's even more.

The early Church Fathers summed up the good news in one incredibly rich, mysterious, and densely packed phrase: "For the Son of God became man so that we might become God."[8]

"Becoming God" is not the heretical claim it might sound like, though it is a phrase meant to shock us into deeper thinking about heaven and holiness. The Fathers called it "deification," or "*theosis.*" Just as a caterpillar is created to undergo a glorious transformation into a butterfly, so humans (even before the fall) were created for a far more glorious, transformative journey into God's own life.

Sin stunted and distorted this journey, of course, and both forgiveness and freedom from sin are now required. But God did not come to earth only as a reaction to human sin. "When the time had fully come" (Galatians 4:4), he came to inaugurate that transformative union with the Creator for which all of creation longs, that the art and the Artist might become one. For each of us, this transformative union begins at Baptism and reaches completion when we behold his glory in Heaven.

Such mysteries are surely beyond our full comprehension. But in *The Grand Miracle*, C. S. Lewis captures a few of the implications for us:

> We are to be remade. . . . [W]e shall find underneath it all a thing we have never yet imagined: a real man, an ageless god, a son of God, strong, radiant, wise, beautiful, and drenched in joy.[9]

- **Does "deification" add anything to your previous understanding of heaven, holiness, or salvation?**

Becoming Myself

Andre

I was sixteen the first time I consciously encountered Jesus in a life-changing way. It was on a high school youth retreat, and there was a Eucharistic procession. As the priest approached, holding the Eucharist, I was suddenly overcome by tears. I wasn't sad or joyful or overwhelmed—I was just crying. I wept freely. Then, after several minutes, a palpable sense of peace came over me such as I had never experienced before and have experienced only seldom since. I *knew* it was God. He was just loving me, being intimately present to me.

When I got home from this retreat, I quit the football team immediately. Not that there's anything wrong with football, but I knew I was playing for the wrong reason: it was what the cool kids did. In the time I would have spent on the football field that fall, I started practicing piano and guitar voraciously. Music eventually became a passion and charism through which I would have the privilege of leading many people to deeper encounters with Christ.

By encountering Jesus, I was "deified" (or sanctified) just a bit more; I became a little more like him, and because of this, I discovered a little more of my true self. A layer of my false self fell off and withered, revealing something better underneath.

The false self is prevalent in all of our lives. We've been hiding behind cleverly crafted fig leaves ever since Eden, afraid of the vulnerability required to trust God's love and God's plan for us.

As God's likeness grows in us over time by grace, we don't become mere copies of one another, but even more resplendent in our diversity. Just as the seemingly infinite array of colors all derive from red, blue, and yellow, so each of God's created persons derives their stunning beauty and uniqueness by union with the Father, Son, and Holy Spirit.

- **What is one way Jesus has removed a fig leaf of your false self?**

6

Free to Respond

Love grows only in an environment
of freedom.

Summary

We began this book by looking at *the gap* we all know too
well. This world isn't all it could or should be. Deep in ourselves, in our very bones, we feel that ache for *something more*.
Consciously or subconsciously, this gap—and the ache it pro-
duces—prompt us to ask, to seek, *to knock*.

What are we searching for? At the surface, answers may
differ widely, but at a sufficient depth, the broad swathe of
humanity seeks the same things: love, joy, peace, and meaning. We share a deep longing for all that is good, true, and
beautiful. We're all searching for God. As Augustine famously
described, "You have made us for yourself, and our heart is
restless until it rests in you."[10]

After looking at the gap, we considered the claim that Jesus proclaims and brings about the definitive "good news"—good news that answers our deepest longings, accounts for the gap, and beckons us toward an adventurous journey with an ultimate fulfillment beyond our wildest imaginations.

The source, center, and summit of this good news is not a philosophy or a moral code but a Person: Jesus Christ himself. He is the one true God; "there is no other" (Isaiah 45:5). No other name, no other figure, and no other power can rescue us from the brokenness of creation and restore us to fullness of life by giving us a share in his own divine life.

And so, we are invited to know that we are **God's beloved** (chapter 2), and though **broken by sin** (chapter 3), we are also **rescued by grace** (chapter 4), which means we are **being transformed** (chapter 5) into all that God has destined us to become. But there's one more basic element of the good news: we are **free to respond.**

Love Requires Freedom.

We follow a God whose very nature is love. Thus, the good news only makes sense within a context of love. And there's something about love that everyone who has ever loved knows: love cannot be forced. It cannot be demanded, coerced, or cajoled. Love requires a free response. It grows only in an environment of freedom.

This reality helps us understand that God will not, *would not*, force us to love him and others. To do so would contradict his own decision to make creatures in his image, capable of genuine, freely chosen love. God does not simply zap us with grace, clean up the mess of the world in one fell swoop, or demand conformity to his will. Though we cannot reach inside his mind (see Isaiah 55:9), we do know at least this much: God is a lover who pursues us relentlessly, and also waits—a painfully long time it may seem—for the free and loving response of his beloved.

It's a principle that runs throughout Catholic faith and theology. God takes the initiative and we respond. Grace moves first. It comes to us in a thousand ways—in every sacrament, in every page of Scripture, in every grace-filled moment with loved ones, in the cry of the poor, and in each glimpse of nature's awe-inspiring beauty. But the flowering of grace in our lives into "fruit that will remain" (John 15:16, NABRE) depends at least somewhat upon our freely chosen cooperation with God. God's yes to us awaits our yes in return. We are unequal partners in a divine-human marriage, fueled by a wooing and winning love that can set the world on fire. What an amazing mystery: God longs to partner with us to bring more of his life into the world!

What Then Shall We Do?

As John the Baptist was preaching and baptizing, many in the crowd responded, "What then shall we do?" (Luke 3:10).

This question is one of the best ever uttered. We hear it again in response to Peter's Pentecost speech to the crowds in Acts 2:37. If we truly hear the good news, we are compelled to ask, "What then shall we do?"

So there it is: What shall we do?

The answer Peter gives to the crowds is to "repent, and be baptized every one of you in the name of Jesus Christ for the forgiveness of your sins; and you shall receive the gift of the Holy Spirit" (Acts 2:38).

"Repent." It's the same word Jesus used upon announcing the proper response to the news that "the kingdom of God is at hand" (Mark 1:15). But we often miss the depth of this word in English, translated from *metanoia* (Greek). It means:

> A change of life . . . that is a profound transformation of mind and heart . . . [that] manifests itself at all levels of the Christian's existence: in his interior life of adoration and acceptance of the divine will, in his action, participation in the mission of the Church, in his married and family life; in his professional life; in fulfilling economic and social responsibilities.[11]

- **Does this definition of "repent" deepen or expand your previous understanding of the word?**

- **In what ways have you experienced some of the richness of repentance (*metanoia*) conveyed here?**

God's Yes to Us

Before we continue with our response to God's invitation to *metanoia*, let's recall the context of this relationship. We are God's beloved children.

When a mother or father first holds their child, vows and commitments swirl around the occasion. Spontaneous sentiments like "I will always love you," "You are mine," and "I am yours" burst out of a parent's heart. At this moment, as well as the nine months before, parents offer a fundamental yes to their child.

If there is one thing that the life, death, and resurrection of Jesus make clear to us, it is that God has given a fundamental yes to his people. At first, he revealed this motherly, fatherly yes to the people of Israel: "I have called you by name, you are mine. . . . [Y]ou are precious in my eyes, . . . and I love you" (Isaiah 43:1, 4). But because of what Christ accomplished and revealed in the fullness of time, we now understand that God's yes is not only for the physical descendants of Abraham but for all who sincerely seek the Lord. In Baptism, then, God's yes to humanity becomes a personal, intimate yes to each of us. God is decidedly for each and every one of us, on our side. He loves each of us with the heart of a mother, a father, a lover, and a friend.

- How have you experienced God's yes to you? Is this something you desire to know and experience more of?

- If you were baptized as an infant, was there a time when you became more consciously aware of the promises and presence of God in your life?

Our Yes to God

How are we to respond to God's firm yes to us?

For starters, we give God what he has given us: our firm yes. Just as he declares to us, so we can say back to him, "I am yours, and you are mine" (see Isaiah 43:1, 5, 15). That's the language of lovers. That's the fragrance of family.

God's yes to us is perfect; our yes to him is not yet perfect. But as we say yes—again and again—to receive his love and mercy, our yes can grow in integrity. We mature in holiness through both grace and effort (and much failure) over a lifetime of learning to say yes.

Such is the process of maturing love in a broken world. A husband and wife, for example, make a firm yes to each other at the altar, even though they have much to learn about love in action. Sometimes this learning comes through hurtful failures to love well. But the vows create a spacious and forgiving freedom within which they can learn to grow in fidelity to the words they spoke at the altar. The firm yes of the vows undergirds and makes possible the entire journey of maturing love.

God's yes to us creates the spacious and forgiving freedom within which we learn to say yes to him.

Solidify Your Yes to God.

The Church calls our basic yes to God the "firm option" (choice) that is "the basis for the whole Christian life of the Lord's disciple." This firm choice "prepares the way for conversion" and "brings with it adherence to Christ and the will to walk in his footsteps."[12]

We might call wedding vows a firm choice of both spouses to love each other "until death do them part." We could say a parent's decision to choose life for a child is an example of a firm choice, which give rise to new life and new relationships.

Is there a moment or season you could point to in your life in which you made a firm choice to say yes to God and follow Jesus?

Whether or not you can recall a decisive moment, it is always good to reaffirm your firm yes to God. One of your moments could be right now.

There is no one formula for doing this of course. It may be a simple prayer from the heart. It may be a brief prayer you write to Jesus in your journal. You might choose to recite, slowly and prayerfully, the Apostles Creed or the Renewal of Baptismal Promises (see next page). Or sing a hymn that expresses your decision and commitment. Perhaps you sit for a few moments of silence, uttering a simple yes to Jesus in the depths of your soul.

To help you, here is one brief prayer you might use. At the end of the first chapter of Pope Benedict's 1968 classic *Introduction to Christianity,* he gives a basic form of the central confession of our faith, which can be a wonderful example of a firm yes to God in Christ:

"I believe in you, Jesus of Nazareth, as the meaning . . . of the world and of my life."[13]

In whatever way is most authentic to you, we invite you to restate this firm choice, this fundamental yes to Jesus Christ in your life. It's not a promise to be perfect today. It's not a vow that you'll never wrestle with doubt or question some teachings of the Church. It is a restatement of the central truth of your life—that Jesus Christ is "the way, and the truth, and the life" (John 14:6).

Renewing Our Baptismal Promises

The Church's Renewal of Baptismal Promises provides a dynamic, compelling way to reaffirm our firm choice for Christ. Consider renewing your own baptismal promises with these words, now or soon:

V. Do you reject Satan?

R. I do.

V. And all his works?

R. I do.

V. And all his empty promises?

R. I do.

V. Do you believe in God, the Father Almighty, creator of heaven and earth?

R. I do.

V. Do you believe in Jesus Christ, his only Son, our Lord, who was born of the Virgin Mary, was crucified, died, and was buried, rose from the dead, and is now seated at the right hand of the Father?

R. I do.

V. Do you believe in the Holy Spirit, the holy Catholic church, the communion of saints, the forgiveness of sins, the resurrection of the body, and life everlasting?

R. I do.

V. God, the all-powerful Father of our Lord Jesus Christ has given us a new birth by water and the Holy Spirit, and forgiven all our sins. May he also keep us faithful to our Lord Jesus Christ for ever and ever.

R. Amen.

God Is Building a Palace.

On this journey so far, we have reflected on the good news of Jesus Christ.[14] God is love. He has reached into our lives to rescue us from darkness, beckoning us to participate in a transformative journey into the fullness of his blessed life. As we say yes—again and again—to God's gracious initiative, we are being transformed (see 2 Corinthians 3:18) into Christ and into our true selves. He is closing the gap.

We used many terms and painted with a broad brush, staying away from more precise distinctions theologians rightly make. So whether you call this grace-filled journey of transformation conversion, *metanoia*, salvation, holiness, or deification (or even something else), you're describing some of the beautiful and mysterious effects of following Jesus.

A wonderful image for this transformative journey of yes comes from C. S. Lewis in *Mere Christianity:*

Imagine yourself as a living house. God comes in to rebuild that house. At first, perhaps, you can understand what He is doing. He is getting the drains right and stopping the leaks in the roof and so on: you knew that those jobs needed doing and so you are not surprised. But presently he starts knocking the house about in a way that hurts abominably and does not seem to make sense. What on earth is He up to? The explanation is that He is building quite a different house from the one you thought of—throwing out a new wing here, putting on an extra floor there, running up towers, making courtyards. You thought you were going to be made into a decent little cottage: but He is building a palace. He intends to come and live in it Himself.[15]

You can trust the Builder. He's doing a magnificent work in you.

PART 2

EXPLORE THE TERRAIN: BASICS OF DISCIPLESHIP

7

Disciple

Being a disciple is not about leveling up from beginner to intermediate Christian. It's about being all in.

New

Andrea

Over ten years ago now, I went on a life-changing retreat and unwrapped the gift of my Baptism. That weekend, I welcomed the power of the resurrection into my heart. I sat in the upper room with the apostles, and Jesus breathed his Spirit on me. I was made new.

I will sprinkle clean water over you to make you clean . . . . I will give you a new heart, and a new spirit I will put within you. I will remove the heart of stone from your flesh and give you a heart of flesh. I will put my spirit within you so that you walk in my statutes, observe my ordinances, and keep them

. . . . You will be my people, and I will be your God (Ezekiel 36:25-28, NABRE).

When I came home—back to my same campus, back to my same dorm room, back to my same roommates—everything was different. I was different. I saw my life with new eyes. I had new understanding and new priorities. I had completely new joy, love, and enthusiasm for life.

Since that day, I've walked on a new trajectory. My "old self" occasionally resurfaces. But that's not me anymore, that old self is not who I am in Christ Jesus. I am a Christ-follower, a disciple. It is a thrilling, beautiful, and satisfying way to live.

Visualize the waters of Baptism being poured onto the top of your head. Imagine that instead of rolling down your face, they go right inside of you, filling you from the toes up like the vessel of the Holy Spirit you are. But along the way, the waters hit little dams and blockades, areas of yourself you haven't yet opened to God.

- **What areas are you holding back?**

- **Are there parts of your life you've walled off from Jesus?**

- **What would it be like to give even one of those over to him?**

Open the gates and let the waters rush in.

Follow

Jesus' disciples came from all walks of life: fishermen, tax collectors, political activists, officials, rich people, those racked with disease, and those with empty stomachs. Yet they all had one thing in common: they *followed* Jesus. This following distinguishes a disciple. Disciples are those who follow where Jesus leads.

Before Christianity was known by that title, early Christians were known as adherents of "the Way." In the Acts of the Apostles, we hear that Paul and his companions created "no little stir concerning the Way" (Acts 19:23). Before Paul's conversion, he sought out "any belonging to the Way, men or women, [that] he might bring them bound to Jerusalem" (9:2).

What is the Way of Jesus?

"Jesus told his disciples, 'If any man would come after me, let him deny himself and take up his cross and follow me'" (Matthew 16:24).

The Way of Jesus is the way of the cross.

"Let us run with perseverance the race that is set before us, looking to Jesus the pioneer and perfecter of our faith, who for the joy that was set before him endured the cross" (Hebrews 12:1-2).

The Way of Jesus leads to joy.

"Simon Peter said to him, 'Lord, where are you going?' Jesus answered, 'Where I am going you cannot follow me now; but . . . I will come again and will take you to myself, that where I am you may be also. And you know the way where I am going.' Thomas said to him, 'Lord, we do not know where you are going; how can we know the way?' Jesus said to him,

'I am the way, and the truth, and the life; no one comes to the Father, but by me'" (John 13:36; 14:3-6).

The Way of Jesus is the way to everlasting life with God.

Jesus invites you, "Come, follow me" (Matthew 4:19, NIV). Are you ready to join him on the Way?

Open Wide.

What comes into your mind or heart when you hear Jesus calling, "Come, follow me"? In his inaugural homily, Pope Benedict addressed the hesitations many feel when contemplating the invitation to follow Jesus:

> Are we not perhaps all afraid in some way? If we let Christ enter fully into our lives, if we open ourselves totally to him, are we not afraid that He might take something away from us? Are we not perhaps afraid to give up something significant, something unique, something that makes life so beautiful? . . . No! If we let Christ into our lives, we lose nothing, nothing, absolutely nothing of what makes life free, beautiful and great. No! Only in this friendship are the doors of life opened wide. Only in this friendship is the great potential of human existence truly revealed. Only in this friendship do we experience beauty and liberation. And so, today, with great strength and great conviction, on the basis of long personal experience of life, I say to you, dear young people: Do not be afraid of Christ! He takes nothing away, and he gives you everything. When we give ourselves to him, we receive a hundredfold in return. Yes, open, open wide the doors to Christ—and you will find true life.[16]

- Are you afraid in any way to let Christ fully enter your life?

- What changes or new experiences give you pause or tempt you to postpone letting Jesus in?

Be honest with yourself and with God about your fears, and let Pope Benedict's words encourage you: "Do not be afraid of Christ!"

All In

Have you ever noticed how often Jesus' disciples don't get it or mess up in the Gospels? A common refrain from Jesus is "Oh, you of little faith!" Yet even as they are figuring it all out, Jesus' followers are disciples. Being a disciple is not about leveling up from beginner to intermediate Christian. It's about being *all in*.

> As they were going along the road, a man said to [Jesus], "I will follow you wherever you go." And Jesus said to him, "Foxes have holes, and birds of the air have nests; but the Son of man has nowhere to lay his head." To another he said, "Follow me." But he said, "Lord, let me first go and bury my father." But he said to him, "Leave the dead to bury their own dead; but as for you, go and proclaim the kingdom of God." Another said, "I will follow you, Lord; but let me first say farewell to those at my home." Jesus said to him, "No one who puts his hand to the plow and looks back is fit for the kingdom of God." (Luke 9:57-62)

Many biblical versions call the people in this passage the "would-be disciples of Jesus." What a heartbreaking phrase "would-be" is! Jesus extends the offer of discipleship to each of these people, they consider it, and they decide something else is more important than following him. These people don't choose to do something inherently evil—they are looking to seek secure shelter, bury a parent, and bid their family farewell—and yet *anything* we choose instead of following Jesus becomes an idol. Choosing something *not Jesus* instead *of Jesus* always means not choosing Jesus.

It's okay if you haven't figured it all out yet, but if you've decided to follow Jesus, don't give yourself any excuse to turn back. Be all in.

A Change in Direction

Andrea

That Greek word *metanoia* we've seen a few times now signifies a fundamentally changed life, "a transformation of mind and heart." When I said yes to Jesus, I experienced his love and mercy in a deep, true way. I was irrevocably changed, converted. But God wasn't done with me yet.

Conversion can happen in big, clear moments, but it is *always* a long-term commitment to transformation.

In the months after my initial moments of conversion, I started noticing lifestyle habits and ways of thinking that didn't line up. I had identified the person I wanted to be—a committed Christ-follower, a disciple—but my habits and inclinations were still stuck in my "old self."

Conversion is a lifelong process of giving more of ourselves to Jesus and allowing him to transform every bit of us. It is the process of becoming fully alive in the identity God designed for us. As I surrender more of myself to Jesus, that gap between who I am in Christ and who I am right now slowly closes.

We keep talking about *the gap*. Sanctification, a movement toward holiness, the change inherent in *metanoia,* closes that gap in us a little.

In this part of the apprenticeship and the next, we will concentrate on cultivating the heart and habits of a disciple. By putting your faith in Jesus, you've taken the first step of discipleship. (And the first step is always the most important one, isn't it?!) These habits and ways of being will help solidify your *metanoia* or conversion, lining up more and more of yourself with the Way of Jesus. They will help you become a disciple in the ways you think, love, walk, talk, and live.

The Discipleship Wheel

Following Jesus is beautifully simple. This illustration of the Discipleship Wheel[17] tries to capture that simplicity and give a glance at the heart and habits of life in Christ. If you incorporate each of the wheel's categories into your life in Christ, your spiritual "wheel" will keep moving you closer to him. These categories identify realistic, concrete areas for ongoing growth in discipleship.

The Hub: Christ at the Center

Jesus, the One who heals, saves, and redeems us, as well as all of humanity, is set firmly at the center of the Wheel and our lives.

Inner Rim: Sacramental Life

The sacraments draw us deeply into the life of Christ through his body, the Church. Thus the sacramental life is drawn in a circle around Christ, the center of our lives. The seven sacraments of the Church are Baptism, Eucharist, Confirmation, Reconciliation, Anointing of the Sick, Matrimony, and Holy Orders.

Vertical Axis: Prayer

Good relationships include spending time together talking and listening. Prayer is the essential means of our relationship with

God, the place where we meet God and experience his love, and both talk and listen to him. As followers of Jesus, we pray communally (for example, at Mass) but also privately, in our inner room. Daily conversations with Jesus foster our relationship with him.

Vertical Axis: Scripture
God communicates his word to us in many ways, but primarily through the Scriptures and the Church. When we read and meditate on God's word—with the help of the Holy Spirit and the lived experience (or tradition) of the Church—we get to know him better and draw closer to him.

Horizontal Axis: Community
The Holy Spirit binds the followers of Jesus together in love. Jesus did not intend for us to be isolated, trying to live discipleship all on our own. We need one another for support, encouragement, and accountability.

Horizontal Axis: Evangelization
The Church exists to announce the good news of Jesus Christ—to evangelize. As we experience Jesus, a natural desire arises in us to share the joy, peace, and love we have found in him with others. We witness to Jesus' good news by how we live, what we say, and how we love others.

Outer Rim: Obedience to Christ and His Church
Obedience, or living out discipleship in our attitudes and actions, keeps it all together. God gives us the Scriptures and the Church to help us know how best to follow him. Everything

God has asked of us is for one purpose: that we might love him and love one another as Christ loves us.

8

Prayer

I got down on my knees and told God I
didn't know what to do.

Beginning to Pray

Clare

I remember the first time I prayed. I was twenty-five years old, and a couple of friends had just given me a Bible and the *Catechism*. I'd been flirting with the faith for months, and these friends had kept witnessing to me. One fall evening, with my apartment windows open, I put those two books on my dresser, and I got down on my knees and told God I didn't know what to do. I hunched over, kind of rolling into myself, eyes shut, and started seeing all these things: people and places and situations in need of healing, in need of attention, in need of . . . prayer. I didn't say anything. I

> just watched the scenes flicker past on that black space of "screen" behind my eyes, and I *loved* those things—those people and places in need of love.

In Hebrew, the word *ruah* means both "breath" and "spirit." It is God's *ruah* that hovers over the waters at creation in Genesis 1. God breathes life in to the human he molded out of dust in Genesis 2. At the end of the Gospel of John, the risen Jesus breathes (*ruah*) on the disciples to fill them with his Holy Spirit and make them new creations. When we pray, Scripture tell us that "the Spirit helps us in our weakness; for we do not know how to pray as we ought, but the Spirit himself intercedes for us with sighs too deep for words" (Romans 8:26).

As you begin to pray, don't worry about doing it "right." You may feel silly or unsure as you start out. In time, prayer will feel more natural. For now, just take a deep breath, open your heart and mind, and settle into the Spirit of God.

So We Need Silence.

> *"Be still, and know that I am God."*
> (Psalm 46:10)

We just talked about settling into the Spirit of God, an activity that may benefit from a little silence. So how do we find that silence? A fellow named Gordon Hempton wrote a book called *One Square Inch of Silence*. In this work, Hempton shows Americans just how hard it is to find true silence today. Cars, airplanes overhead, reverberations from heavy machinery, and so many other "conveniences" make finding real silence close to impossible for most people.

But God wants us to "be still" and to sit and know him that way—in stillness. Yes, it's hard. Very hard. On top of kids, the cell phone, the coworker who needs something, a school assignment if that's where you are right now, date night (which you know you need to honor!), the laundry, that new song you love, and the ring of the microwave as it finishes warming up those leftovers, there is the interior roar of thoughts, to-dos, plans, worries, and daydreams.

Is there a way to find silence, to find stillness, even for five minutes each day, to sit with God? To unplug and just sit with him. Is it possible? Is it possible to get out of bed in the dark just a few minutes earlier, to sit on the floor with the light just creeping past the blinds, and feel him with us? Or maybe we could sit in the car, within that dark garage, for five minutes before we open that overhead door and let in the day.

How can we find silence, stillness, and rest with God today?

Quiet Time with God

How to Spend Quiet Time with God

Begin by recognizing that God is with you, even when you're not paying attention. When you attend to God, you are simply focusing on reality.

In *The Book of Her Life*, St. Teresa of Avila called prayer "an intimate sharing between friends."[18] Any good friendship involves three things: talking, listening, and simply being together, right? Think about the time you spend, and have spent, with close friends: with the woman who was the maid of honor at your wedding or with the man who is your son's godfather.

Talk to God

There is *no* wrong way to talk to God. Talk about anything on your mind. Keep it real; don't say what you think a prayerful person "should" say or what you think God wants to hear. Even saying "Lord, help me to pray" is prayer.

In Part I, we had that story about James and his father and son, that idea of God seeing us the way loving parents see their children. As children, we (hopefully!) learned a few basic phrases: "Thank you," "I'm sorry," "please." There's a great outline for a chat with God!

Listen to God

> *"Morning by morning he wakens, / he wakens my ear / to hear as those who are taught."*
> (Isaiah 50:4)

No matter how impossible it may seem, you can learn to hear the Lord's voice in your life. Remember the promise of Jesus: "My sheep hear my voice, and I know them, and they follow me" (John 10:27). The fastest way to learn to recognize God's voice is to read the Scriptures prayerfully (more on that later). With the Holy Spirit coming to our aid, the word becomes a life-giving encounter with God.

Be with God

Sometimes words get in the way of deeper communication. St. John of the Cross said, "The Father spoke one Word, which was his Son, and this Word he speaks always in eternal silence, and in silence must it be heard by the soul."[19] And as we discussed just a little while ago, the Lord says, "Be still, and know that I am God" (Psalm 46:10).

Begin and end your prayer time with a minute or two of silence. Rest in God's presence. You may not hear anything or even sense anything interiorly, but know that God is filling this silence. Often, a concern can gain clarity later in the day after a time of silence in the morning.

What Do I Talk about in Prayer?

Your life!

It's that easy (and, perhaps, that hard).

God the Father wants to hear about the lives of his children. Jesus wants to hear about your life.

Prayer can start with recognition of God's greatness: "Father, you are good." God created us. As the *Catechism* explains, adoration comes with acknowledging that we are creatures before our Creator (see 2628). We can exult the greatness of the Lord who created us, the power of the savior who sets us free from evil. As stained as the world is, it may be difficult to *feel* adoration at all times (we may feel angry toward God or confused by things in our lives that obscure for us God's pure goodness, and that's okay), but we can use prayer to come back to the truth of God's ever greater presence.

As we praise God, we can apologize for our mistakes. In expressing contrition, we humble ourselves and purify our prayer (see *Catechism*, 2631).

Then we can thank God, thank Jesus, for all the blessings we have already received. Cultivating gratitude gives us perspective and reminds us again of God's goodness, even in the midst of difficulty.

And, of course, we can ask for anything and everything we need in our lives. Big or small, he wants to hear about our needs, hopes, wishes, and desires. So often in popular culture, people express derision for those who pray for "things," suggesting we should not ask God to help us with material needs. But, as the *Catechism* explains, we *turn back to God* by petitioning him (see 2629).

Likewise, we can and should ask God to help others, from the leaders of our country to the coworker with whom we struggle.

Easily call to mind the four movements of prayer described above with the acronym ACTS:

A doration
C ontrition
T hanksgiving
S upplication

Bring anything and everything into your conversations with God! And if you are looking for a structure to guide your prayer time, give ACTS a shot.

Practice: Schedule Daily Prayer

Andrea

If we have an appointment on the calendar, we go. If the class is scheduled, we show up. If the party starts at 8 p.m., we're there. Scheduling a regular appointment with God helps many people develop a habit of prayer. A scheduled time makes prayer a priority, and clearly shows whether we kept our appointment or missed it. Scheduling can sound like "every day at 7 a.m." or like "for fifteen minutes immediately before lunch" even if lunchtime varies every day.

Many people prefer praying and listening to God first thing in the morning before the activity (and unpredictability!) of the day sets in, but pray how and when you can. It's more important to schedule a time each day than to schedule an ideal time you won't keep.

I encourage you to spend this time *exclusively* with God in one uninterrupted period—not while driving or doing other activities. In Part 3, we'll talk about "praying at all times" by adding prayer to different parts of our day, but for now, concentrate on forming the habit of focusing solely on God during your scheduled prayer time.

If you miss a day, don't get discouraged; just get back on track. Instead of beating yourself up over a missed appointment, consider it part of the process of forming the habit. If you miss a session, or even two, explore why you missed that appointment, and create a strategy to overcome those obstacles in the future. Some people log completed prayer times in a habit tracker or ask a friend for accountability to help them solidify their prayer practice.

So get out your calendar (digital or paper) and schedule in your prayer time for each day this week! Reminders such as phone notifications, a sticky note on your lunch box, or other triggers (I always pray with my first cup of coffee in the morning) can help you keep your commitment to regularly scheduled prayer.

9

Eucharist

Here I was, coming to Mass to grow closer to Jesus, and I just couldn't focus.

Grocery Lists and Eucharistic Prayers

Andrea

When I was in college, I experienced a season of conversion when I felt drawn to commit myself more deeply to Jesus and to discipleship. I grew up Catholic, but we had never talked about prayer or Scripture at home. I had a Bible and a rosary . . . and not a clue what to do with either. But this desire to go deeper kept drawing me. All I could think to do was to go to Mass.

The familiar rhythms of call and response from the priest and the people would wash over me, and I knew I was in the right place to grow closer to God. But then—two heads of broccoli, a dozen eggs, oatmeal . . . no, actually, the oatmeal will last through the week, coffee, definitely coffee, is that it? Hmm . . . . Oh, shoot! Jolted back to attention by the movement of the priest as he bent to pick up the bread for the consecration, I realized I'd been distracted all through the long, poetic Eucharistic prayer.

I felt awful. Here I was, coming to Mass to grow closer to Jesus, and I just couldn't focus. The rhythms of Mass were familiar, but I had a sneaking suspicion that maybe I didn't really get what was happening. I believed the Mass was really important, but I couldn't have told you why.

• What role has Mass played in your life of discipleship?

• What significance does it have for you?

• Do you struggle with boredom or distraction?

Praying the Mass

Andrea

I knew I wasn't being drawn to Mass just to compose my grocery list every Sunday.

In a desperate act to stay focused, I began mentally repeating every word the priest said. In the battle against the grocery list, I took up as much thought territory as possible with the words of the Mass. The result surprised me.

Words I had spoken thoughtlessly began to gain meaning.

I recited, "But only say the word and my soul shall be healed" and wondered, "what word, Lord? Won't you say it and heal me?" "Jesus is the Word of God," the thought, like a response, flashed into my mind. God *has* spoken. I *am* healed. Wow!

I noticed that the priest always paused before the repetition of *Lord, have mercy. Christ, have mercy. Lord, have mercy.* He was waiting for me to bring to mind any sins I wanted forgiven. I was actually supposed to do something in that pause. Huh!

Over time, the words didn't just wash over me. Instead, they penetrated me and evoked a response. I wasn't just showing up for Mass, I was *praying* the Mass: presenting my offerings, giving thanks, entering into communion, and receiving strength for mission.

In the next few pages, we'll look at the Mass from these four angles (presenting our offerings, giving thanks, entering into communion, and receiving strength for mission).[20] It won't be a play-by-play explanation of the Mass or an exploration into its historical or theological significance. Instead, we'll aim to enter into the prayer of the Mass more deeply.

Offering

Jesus' whole life was an offering of love to God the Father. Free to do anything with his life, Jesus only wanted to do God's saving work: "From the first moment of his Incarnation the Son embraces the Father's plan of divine salvation.

. . . The sacrifice of Jesus 'for the sins of the whole world' [1 John 2:2] expresses his loving communion with the Father" (*Catechism*, 606).

Before he was arrested and crucified, Jesus spent his last meal with his disciples. At this Last Supper, Jesus "took bread, and when he had given thanks, he broke it, and said, 'This is my body which is for you. Do this in remembrance of me'" (1 Corinthians 11:23-24). He gave us his body and blood on the cross and gives them to us every time we celebrate the Eucharist.

We too are called to offer ourselves to God as we follow Jesus. Like Jesus, we can offer our everyday lives to God in our work, our play, our sufferings, our joys, our time with family and friends. When we come to Mass, we bring all of that with us and place it on the altar beside the bread and wine. "The lives of the faithful, their praise, sufferings, prayer, and work, are united with those of Christ and with his total offering, and so acquire a new value. Christ's sacrifice present on the altar makes it possible for all generations of Christians to be united with his offering" (*Catechism*, 1368).

Jesus offers all that he has and all that he is to God. We are called to do the same. At Mass we join our offerings to the sacrificial offering Jesus makes. As we grow in faithfulness, we strive to offer more of ourselves to God in all aspects of our lives.

Eucharistia

Andrea

As a kid, I loved giving my friends elaborate gifts. I would either make them myself or find the perfect thing at the store. At some point, someone asked, "Shouldn't you only give things to people who will give you something too?" It hadn't occurred to me. I just liked giving gifts! But as an adult, I have felt the embarrassment of receiving a gift from someone I didn't get anything for. I feel bad, like I owe them, like we're not on equal footing.

Faced with all the Lord has done for me, I definitely feel on unequal footing. How could I possibly give God something as good as he's given me? How could I even say an adequate "Thank you"? "Thank you" doesn't begin to express the gratitude appropriate for the gift of healing and salvation that the Lord has given.

"How can I repay the LORD / for all the great good done for me? / I will raise the cup of salvation / and call on the name of the LORD" (Psalm 116:12-13, NABRE). "Eucharist" springs from the Greek word *eucharistia,* meaning "thanksgiving." I cannot repay the Lord, but there is one who can. Jesus, in lifting the cup of salvation and calling on God the Father, truly in lifting up his body and blood as the cup of salvation, adequately and wondrously repays God for all that God has given. Jesus is the only gift worthy of the Father, the gift of Jesus' own whole, blameless life, given freely in love of the Father and for us.

As the priest prays, "It is truly right and just, our duty and our salvation, always and everywhere to give you thanks, Father most Holy, through your beloved Son," I take heart. I join my thanksgiving to this gift of Jesus in his life, death, and resurrection. I do so inadequately and hesitantly. But as I take part in the Eucharist, I am transformed further into the life of Christ. Slowly but surely, I begin to live my life as an act of thanksgiving, always and everywhere, all for God's glory alone.

- **What are three things you are grateful for today?**

- **Offer your thanks to God.**

Communion

Jesus' followers often wrestled with the strangeness of his words. He said some shocking things. When Jesus told his followers that his body was "true food" and his blood was "true drink" (John 6:55, NABRE), his disciples responded with: "This is a hard saying; who can listen to it?" (6:60). Jesus pressed them further: "Do you take offense at this?" (6:61). After many people left him, Jesus turned to the Twelve, saying, "Will you also go away?" (6:67).

Believing that the Eucharist is Jesus—Body, Blood, Soul, and Divinity—takes as much faith today as it did then. But since the earliest times, the Church has proclaimed that Jesus "was known to them in the breaking of the bread" (Luke 24:35). We encounter Christ's *true presence* in the Eucharist.

God's great desire is for us to be with him. He sent his son to bridge the gap of sin and brokenness. While sin puts something between us and God, Communion is the opposite—nothing comes between us; we enjoy radical closeness to God. "The principal fruit of receiving the Eucharist in Holy Communion is an intimate union with Christ Jesus" (*Catechism*, 1391).

Jesus told his followers that he was true food and drink, not to shock them or to drive them away, but to assure them that he alone was the source of their life. He offered them a closeness they could hardly conceive of. "He who eats my flesh and drinks my blood abides in me, and I in him. As the living Father sent me, and I live because of the Father, so he who eats me will live because of me" (John 6:56-57). When the minister of the Eucharist lifts the host before you at Mass and declares, "The Body of Christ," they are not announcing only the true substance of what they offer you; they are declaring the true substance of each of us who receives the Eucharist. Bread is transformed, and so is Christ's church. We are the body of Christ.

Draw near to Christ. He offers you true food, true drink, and true life. Let him dwell within you. His very presence will transform you.

Food for Mission

The word "Mass" comes from the Latin word *missa*, "sent." At the end of Mass, the priest sends us into the world: "Go in peace, glorifying the Lord by your life." Having brought to the altar all the stuff of our lives—sufferings, anxieties, thanksgivings, petitions, praise—we are transformed by communion with God and with our fellow worshippers. And then we are sent in peace to continue Jesus' work of healing and saving the world. The God who became human—and the dead One who became alive—now becomes *food for us*, so that we might become life-saving food for the world.

Eucharist is food for *mission*.

Pope Benedict XVI called us to greater "eucharistic consistency," that our worship would overflow into deeper love for our neighbor. "The love that we celebrate in the sacrament is not something we can keep to ourselves. By its very nature it demands to be shared with all."[21]

When Mary received the Word of God and Jesus was conceived in her womb, she set out and traveled "with haste" to her cousin Elizabeth (Luke 1:39). Arriving at Elizabeth's house, Mary announced, "My soul proclaims the greatness of the Lord; / my spirit rejoices in God my savior. / For he has looked upon his handmaid's lowliness; / behold, from now on will all ages call me blessed. / The Mighty One has done great things for me, / and holy is his name" (1:46-49, NABRE). Scripture goes on to mention the detail that Mary stayed with Elizabeth for about three months before returning home, long enough to assist her older cousin with the birth of John the Baptist (Luke 1:56). Having received the Word of God, Mary goes and glorifies the Lord in her words and her deeds. She exhibited perfect "eucharistic consistency."

- **What is one small way in which your life might exhibit a better "eucharistic consistency"?**

- **Where are you being sent with the love of Jesus?**

Practice: Prepare for the Celebration of the Eucharist

Andrea

A professor of mine once talked about the great procession of the church to the celebration of the Eucharist: mothers wiping faces and encouraging children to try going one last time; fathers scraping frost off cold car windows; kids finding and losing mittens, struggling with zippers; widows carefully donning hats and overcoats; matrons with meticulously coifed white hair; students closing laptops on this week's project. Finding the parking space, walking the block or two, signing the cross with holy water, carefully choosing a pew or plunking down in the nearest open spot. One and all processing toward the Lord's altar.

How do you prepare to approach the altar of the Lord?

In this section, we reflect on four ways to pray with the Mass: presenting your offering, giving thanks, entering into communion, and receiving strength for our mission. As you make your own procession to the altar, reserve some time to prepare your heart and mind for Jesus.

Preparing Your Offering

Arrive a few minutes before Mass to collect yourself physically, mentally, and spiritually. Consider what you bring to Mass today:

- What's happened since the last time you were at Mass?
- What joys or sorrows are on your heart?
- What events/experiences in work, student, or family life do you bring?
- Who or what are you praying for today?

Bring them all as an offering to the Lord.

Preparing Your Thanksgiving

Along with your offering, cultivate gratitude in your heart. Either before Mass or with your reception of the Eucharist, express your gratitude to God for all the good done to you: the big things—salvation, God's love, friends, family—and all the little things too.

Preparing for Communion

The *Catechism* (1394) describes the strength the Eucharist gives us for maintaining communion: "As bodily nourishment restores lost strength, so the Eucharist strengthens our charity, which tends to be weakened in daily life. . . . By giving himself to us Christ revives our love and enables us to break our disordered attachments to creatures and root ourselves in him."

Before we are ready for the remarkable communion Jesus offers in the Eucharist, we must seek healing of any major divisions between us and the Lord (mortal sins) in the Sacrament of Reconciliation (more on this coming up). As you prepare yourself for Mass, call to mind any venial sins and ask forgiveness.

Preparing for Mission

How is the Lord calling you to bring the love and communion experienced at Mass out to the whole world? Each of us is called to be life-saving food for the world through our words and actions, like Mary carrying the Bread of Life within us as we go forth from the doors of the church.

Prepare for the priest or deacon's commission to "go in peace, glorifying the Lord by your life." Ask for whatever graces and strength you need to carry out the particular mission Jesus has placed on your heart.

10

Word of God

Through the Holy Spirit, the ancient words
speak directly to our hearts.

Word Made Flesh

God speaks special words. They not only carry ideas, but they
make stuff happen. "God said, 'Let there be light'; and there
was light" (Genesis 1:3). Jesus "rebuked the wind, and said to
the sea, 'Peace! Be still!' And the wind ceased, and there was
a great calm" (Mark 4:39). God compares his word to rain
and snow, not falling aimlessly but rather watering the earth.
"So shall my word be / that goes forth from my mouth; / it
shall not return to me empty, / but shall do what pleases me, /
achieving the end for which I sent it" (Isaiah 55:11, NABRE).
God's word is not only *communicative*; it is *performative*. It
achieves what God intends.

God's word is reality itself: so real it is a divine Person—Jesus, the Word made flesh (see John 1:14). More than any speech, Jesus himself communicates God's message of love, reconciliation, and rescue to us. The Word of God achieves what God intends.

Prayerfully consider this passage from the Gospel of Luke (7:2, 6-10):

> Now a centurion had a slave who was dear to him, who was sick and at the point of death. . . . When [Jesus] was not far from the house, the centurion sent friends to him, saying to him, "Lord, do not trouble yourself, for I am not worthy to have you come under my roof; therefore I did not presume to come to you. But say the word, and let my servant be healed. For I am a man set under authority, with soldiers under me: and I say to one, 'Go,' and he goes; and to another, 'Come,' and he comes; and to my slave, 'Do this,' and he does it." When Jesus heard this he marveled at him, and turned and said to the multitude that followed him, "I tell you, not even in Israel have I found such faith." And when those who had been sent returned to the house, they found the slave well.

Jesus commends the centurion's immense faith—he believed completely in the performative power of Jesus' word. If Jesus said it, it would happen. He believed in Jesus' authority, even over death. Believe. God's word has power.

The Voice of God

Andrea

If I were to lose my sight tomorrow, I'm confident I would be able to distinguish my husband's voice from the voices of others. I know it so well—his cadences, word choices, intonations, and tenor. I am so familiar with him that his words communicate more to me than an acquaintance speaking the same phrases. Our familiarity allows him to communicate *himself* through each word. I hear what he's saying and what he's not saying. I *know* him, his heart, his intentions. That knowledge informs how I understand his words.

In the earlier chapter on prayer, we suggested that the best way to learn to recognize God's voice is to read the Scriptures prayerfully. The Scriptures increase our familiarity with the Person of God by leading us to contemplate the things he did and said throughout history, and in particular in the Person of Jesus. St. Jerome famously said, "Ignorance of the Scriptures is ignorance of Christ." All the Gospels' accounts of Jesus and his disciples help us to see the sort of person (and God) he is.

Reading and praying with Scripture nourishes our relationship with God through an exchange of words. "We only devote periods of quiet time to the things or the people whom we love; and here we are speaking of the God whom we love, a God who wishes to speak to us. . . . 'Speak, LORD, for your servant is listening' (1 Samuel 3:9)" (*Evangelii Gaudium*, 146). The Church affirms that "in the sacred books, the Father who is in heaven meets His children with great love and speaks with them" (*Dei Verbum*, 21).

With the Holy Spirit coming to our aid, reading the Scriptures becomes a life-giving encounter with God, "for the word of God is living and active" even now (Hebrews 4:12). While the words themselves are informative, it is not enough merely to read Scripture. When we pray with Scripture, the Holy Spirit equips us with that familiarity that communicates more than the words themselves signify. Through the Holy Spirit the ancient words speak directly to our hearts and to our unique situations.

The Heart of God

St. Gregory the Great wrote this exhortation to a close friend encouraging him to read the Sacred Scriptures:

> I must direct a complaint to you, illustrious son Theodore. Freely you have received from the Most Blessed Trinity intelligence and temporal goods, mercy and love. But you are immersed in material occupations, obliged to travel frequently, and you fail to read daily the words of the Redeemer. Is not Sacred Scripture a letter from almighty God to creation? If you were separated for a time from the emperor and received a letter from him, you would not rest or sleep till you had read what an earthly emperor had written. The Emperor of heaven, the Lord of humanity and angels, has sent you a letter regarding your life, and you fail to read it fervently. I beg of you, apply yourself daily to meditating on the words of your Creator. *Learn to know the heart of God in the words of God*, so that you may tend with greater ardor to things eternal, so that your mind may excite itself to greater desire for heavenly joys.[22]

- What does St. Gregory's exhortation stir up in you? Take any fears, resolutions, or desires to God in prayer.

Context

Andrea

In a world where news is tweeted, I struggle to remember the importance of *context*. What's the story beyond the sound bite? Who are the players we're not hearing from? Where were they when everything went down? What came before the event in question?

Context is everything.

Having gone to Mass for years, I had heard both the story of Herod beheading John the Baptist and of Jesus feeding a crowd of five thousand. But I had no idea one came immediately after the other! (See Matthew 14:1-21.) Reading these stories in context for the first time, I remember sensing the sorrow of Jesus, whose friend and relative Herod had violently killed. I wondered if the crowd searched for Jesus in the midst of their own mourning. What was the mood as he healed and fed the people?

The *Catechism* has three guidelines for reading Scripture in context (see paragraphs 112-114).

1. Consider the passage in light of the *"content and unity of the whole Scripture"* (*Dei Verbum*, 12). Scripture contains many different types of books, but God's plan, with Jesus Christ at the center, unifies them (*Cathechism*, 112).

2. "Read the Scripture with 'the living Tradition of the whole Church.' Sacred Scripture is written principally in the Church's heart rather than in documents and records, for the Church carries in her Tradition the living memorial of God's Word, and it is the Holy Spirit who gives her the spiritual interpretation of the Scripture" (*Catechism*, 113).

3. Think about the "truths of faith" Scripture conveys in itself and "within the whole plan of Revelation" (*Cathechism*, 114).

If you're new to praying with Scripture, it'll take you a while to gain context. That's okay; just keep reading, keep seeking to understand what seems odd or difficult (you can turn to others for help), and, over time, you'll get it.

Speak, Lord

Kendra

They say it's inevitable, but I avoided losing someone I loved for twenty-six years. Then, only months after I moved across the country, leaving all family and familiarity behind me, it happened. My grandmother passed away. "But she was my best friend," I whispered as I wept.

My heart rode agonizing waves of pain, suffering, anger, and sadness. I went to Mass the night she died, and the word proclaimed pierced my soul. As I recited the prayers and mumbled the words of the Nicene Creed, I was pummeled with the stark realities of life and death, heaven and hell, living, dying, and rising. Jesus.

I was not unaffected. All at once, it was personal.

Romans 8:38-39 filled my mind, "For I am sure that neither death, nor life, nor angels, nor principalities, nor things present, nor things to come, nor powers, nor height, nor depth, nor anything else in all creation, will be able to separate us from the love of God in Christ Jesus our Lord."

Nothing. Not even death.

Jesus' victory over death meant that my grandma was met with open arms. And I remembered, moments before she died, she reached her arms upward and fixed her eyes on something or—I thought, as the consoling waves of Jesus' presence soothed me—on Someone.

Into the unpredictability of my grief, Jesus spoke his sure promises: "The Spirit of the LORD GOD is upon me, / . . . to comfort all who mourn; . . . / to give them a garland instead of ashes, / the oil of gladness instead of mourning, / the mantle of praise instead of a faint spirit" (Isaiah 61:1, 2, 3). "My sheep hear my voice, and I know them, and they follow me; and I give them eternal life, and they shall never perish, and no one shall snatch them out of my hand" (John 10:27-28).

I still grieved for my grandma, but as the words of Scripture poured over me, something changed. Now, even in the sadness, I had hope.

Divine Reading

More a library than a book, the Bible is an ancient compilation written over a span of some thousand years by various authors, in multiple genres and languages. Any such collection would contain complexity. (We'll consider some of the subtleties of authorship and interpretation in the chapter on Scripture in Part 3).

The Bible is hardly an "easy read" on every page. Yet the complexity shouldn't keep us from approaching the Bible altogether. Unfortunately, many Catholics keep their distance from the Sacred Scriptures. Among many other reasons, a basic lack of confidence holds many back from seeking God's voice in the Scriptures.

We don't need to be expert scholars or theologians to understand Scripture. The way to start is simple: just dive in!

Will we need some guidance from the Church here and there to ensure we don't get off track? Sure! Will the complexity dumbfound us sometimes? Absolutely! Will difficulties ever tempt us to give up? Count on it. But as we dive into Scripture, our hunger to understand it—with our heads and our hearts—will grow. The Holy Spirit comes to our aid when we approach Scripture with faith.

One way to begin praying with Scripture is the ancient tradition of *lectio divina,* Latin for "divine reading." Many popes and saints have recommended the practice, including Pope Benedict:

> I would like in particular to recall and recommend the ancient tradition of *lectio divina*: the diligent reading of Sacred Scripture accompanied by prayer brings about that intimate dialogue

in which the person reading hears God who is speaking, and in praying, responds to him with trusting openness of heart. (cf. *Dei Verbum*, 25)[23]

We introduce this method in the next section.

Practice: *Lectio Divina*

A special technique for praying with Scripture called *lectio divina* ("divine reading") provides a guide for prayer, meditation, and conversation with God. It forces us to slow ourselves (and our prayers) down, so we can *absorb* Scripture and spend time with God. *Lectio divina* involves a deliberate balance of action and reception, praying and listening to God.

A quick tip: use these 4 Rs as a guide, *not* a constraint. Drift back and forth between different Rs, or jump around. Think of the Rs as having an organic flow, like any good conversation. Focus on God and God's word; let this method enrich your prayer.

Get Ready

Open your Bible—a real Bible whenever possible! The book itself inspires quiet prayerfulness, as opposed to the inherent distractions of most devices.

Choose a short passage, typically one that contains fewer than ten verses, sometimes as few as three. Most Bibles include useful heading breaks to designate topics or narratives within a chapter. If you're new to reading Scripture, we suggest starting with a Gospel like Matthew or Mark, and/or with the Book of Psalms.

Begin with the sign of the cross, and take a moment to get quiet and still. Ask the Holy Spirit to guide your time of prayer.

Read

Read the Scripture selection slowly and attentively. Is there any word, phrase, or image that catches your attention? Make a note of it. Reading a passage multiple times or out loud helps many people focus. Doing this may draw your attention to new elements as well, especially if you are reading a familiar text.

Reflect

Think about the meaning of whatever caught your attention. The Holy Spirit drew you to it for a reason! What does the passage make you think about? Perhaps imagine yourself in the scene. What is the Lord saying to you through this text?

Notice any questions that arise or any emotions you experience. This is often the way God draws your attention to something. Return to the text as often as you wish. Look for any promises to claim, commands to obey, examples to follow, errors to avoid, or praises to sing.

Respond

Talk to God about the passage or anything else on your heart. Thank him for blessings received. Ask him to provide for your needs and those of others. Note any actions you want to live out, and ask God to help you keep your resolutions.

Rest

Rest a few minutes in silence with the Lord. We arrive again at the idea of stillness: "Be still, and know that I am God" (Psalm 46:10).

11

Community

Following Jesus is not a solo sport.

Relentlessly Communal

Christian discipleship is *relentlessly communal*.

God created us in his image and likeness . . . and his very nature is that of a dynamic relationship of love! As difficult as the Trinity is to understand, one of its implications is profoundly simple: we were *made* for relationships.

So on the one hand, the love of Jesus propels us into communion with others. "By this all . . . will know that you are my disciples, if you have love for one another" (John 13:35).

On the other hand, we need the love and support of community to find Jesus in the first place—and to *keep* finding and following him. Throughout salvation history, God has chosen to reveal himself most clearly within the context *of a community*. In the words of Jesus, "For where two or three are gathered in my name, there am I in the midst of them" (Matthew 18:20).

This does not detract from the personal dimension of discipleship. Faith is a deeply personal matter but not a private one.

- Many receive the first seeds of faith and virtue in the community of family.

- The presence of God unites us in the communal rites of liturgy and sacrament.

- The pope and bishops guide our understanding of the mysteries of faith.

- Religious communities witness to the radical demands of the gospel through communal lives of prayer, service, poverty, chastity, and obedience.

- Many laypeople live out discipleship "two by two" through the sacrament of marriage.

- The prayer Jesus taught us begins with "Our."

- Jesus said he is mystically present in the gathered community (see Matthew 18:20), as well as in those who are poor (see Matthew 25:31-46).

- Our community is not even limited to those we can see and hear, but extends to saints and angels in heaven.

Following Jesus is not a solo sport. God is not a Lone Ranger God, and neither are we to be Lone Ranger Christians. We stand on the shoulders of all who have gone before us. We have a critical role to play for those who will come after us. And along the way, we're "surrounded by so great a cloud of witnesses" (Hebrews 12:1). It's far too tough a journey to go it alone.

We need others.

Others need us.

God made us that way.

Together

Andrea

"Honey, you need to get up. It's 6:30."

"But it's Saturday . . ."

"You're getting coffee with Eliza this morning, remember?"

When I was younger, getting together with friends was easy, natural, a regular part of the rhythm of my life. We'd get lunch together, walk to class together, stay up late studying. As an adult, forming and keeping friendships requires me to exercise *intentionality*. I don't share a commute with anyone, lunch isn't a leisurely social event, and I'm too tired to stay up late doing much of anything!

But I know better than to let friendships fall away altogether, especially those relationships I have with other disciples. The Book of Sirach describes a friend as a "sturdy shelter: / he that has found one has found a treasure. / There is nothing so precious as a faithful friend, / and no scales can measure his excellence. / A faithful friend is an elixir of life; / and those who fear the Lord will find him. / Whoever fears the Lord directs his friendship aright, / for as he is, so is his neighbor also" (6:14-17).

I get up at 6:30 a.m. on a Saturday because Eliza needs my friendship and I need hers. We nestle into the coffee shop, her four-month-old sleeping comfortably in her arms. Both of us have given up the slow, gentle start of a Saturday morning to be here, together.

We talk about everything—jobs, husbands, kids, worries, recipes—but the strength of our relationship is found in this simple, profound question: "What has God been doing in your life lately?"

With that question, we tap into the bond that joins us together: our walk with Christ. The question pushes our conversation beyond the surface to the deep places where God is working. Sometimes, it can feel really vulnerable to share about fears or temptations we're dealing with. Other times, we encourage one another with the peace or confidence Jesus has been giving us.

I need Eliza's example and support in order to keep walking with Jesus. I can't do it alone. I have to do it together.

Heart of the Father

Jesus revealed clearly that God is the good, loving, perfect Father of all. Jesus even called the Father "Abba," which is an intimate Aramaic word, like "Dad" or "Daddy."[24] We seek to understand the Father's heart for his children so we might come to share more fully in his love for others—and for ourselves.

Some of God's children are especially weighed down—by life circumstances, their own sin, the sins of others, or some combination of these. God's heart aches in loving concern for those who suffer and struggle. As we follow the Lord, we share his great compassion for his beloved and burdened children.

The Bible often uses the Greek word *splanchna*—translated variously as compassion, tender mercy, and affection—to describe Jesus' reaction to people in need.

> *Splanchna* implies a physical component. It is a deep emotion that makes one's stomach turn over. Jesus is physically and emotionally moved by suffering; his heart obviously bleeds in the presence of poor people, rejected, abandoned, and crushed, who trust in God, but are like sheep without shepherds. He suffers with all those who are in pain, no matter what class, religious group, or nationality they may be. There is something in him that cannot stand hypocrisy and downright injustice to the lowly, to the crippled, to the sick people in need, crippled too in their hearts, filled with guilt and shame.[25]

The *splanchna* of the Son is the heart of the Father, broken for those beaten down by human sinfulness. As followers of Jesus, we are both the sick in need of divine healing, and the physician's assistants helping restore a wounded world.

Compassion

In modern use, the word "compassion" implies a consciousness of the suffering of others. Originally, however, it went much further. The Latin roots mean *to suffer with another*. In some uses in Middle English, it carried this meaning: to actually, literally suffer *with* another.

Jesus consistently had compassion for the crowds and for individuals. Yet he didn't just rush in to "save the day" and offer healings and miracles. He took the time to look people in the eye, to converse with them, to ask them questions, and to listen to their responses. It was as if he knew that they needed more than miracles. They needed to be seen, to be known, to be heard. They needed to feel his loving care and presence. Henri Nouwen describes our experience of this tension in the words "care" and "cure":

> Our tendency is to run away from the painful realities or to try to change them as soon as possible. But cure without care makes us into rulers, controllers, manipulators, and prevents a real community from taking shape. Cure without care makes us preoccupied with quick changes, impatient and unwilling to share each other's burden. And so cure can often become offending instead of liberating.[26]

In the eleventh chapter of John's Gospel, Jesus visits Martha and Mary in Bethany, a few days after their brother Lazarus has died. The women, grieving and wrestling with understandable bitterness, do not hold back their frustrations, even blaming Jesus for not intervening to prevent their brother's death. Both Martha and Mary, within a few verses of each other, say to

Jesus, "Lord, if you had been here, my brother would not have died" (John 11:21, 32).

What did Jesus do? Did he scold them for talking that way to the Messiah? Did he get on with the miracle to avoid a tense moment? Did he defend himself, giving reasons for his "late" arrival in Bethany?

No.

In the shortest verse in Scripture, we read "Jesus wept" (John 11:35).

He suffered with the sisters.

Jesus, who knew the end of the story and was eager to offer a "cure" that would last far beyond the moment, throughout the ages, and would signal the greatest "cure" possible—the resurrection—paused in the moment and wept with his friends.

His friends were weeping, and "if one member suffers, all suffer together" (1 Corinthians 12:26). This is what it means to be a family. It's what it means to be a Church. Care comes before cure.

Son of God, Son of Mary

Baptism initiates us into the family of God. We become sons and daughters "in the Son."[27] Because we share Jesus' sonship, we also share his relationship with his mother, Mary. Through grace and the sacraments, everything Jesus has becomes ours. We do not worship Mary; we show her special honor and appreciation—as sons and daughters do with their earthly mothers.

The early Church Fathers would speak of the *totus Christus,* the "whole Christ," when referring to the Church, the Mystical Body of Christ. To separate Jesus Christ from Christians would be to separate the head from the body. In conceiving Jesus Christ, then, Mary conceived the whole Christ, the Redeemer *and* the redeemed, the head *and* the body.

When she gave her *fiat* ("Let it be to me according to your word," Luke 1:38), Mary lovingly consented to be the mother of the Redeemer and mother of all those who would be redeemed—you and I and all Christians.[28]

> Jesus is Mary's only son, but her spiritual motherhood extends to all men whom indeed he came to save: "The Son whom she brought forth is he whom God placed as the first-born among many brethren, that is, the faithful in whose generation and formulation she cooperates with a mother's love."[29]

In the same way you can talk to your earthly mother (or even if that relationship is strained), you have your heavenly mother to talk to about the needs of the Church, the world, and your life. Ask favors from her; ask for her advice or wisdom; seek her as someone to listen to. Entrust those needs to her maternal care. She'll bring them to Jesus.

Practice: Spiritual Friendship

Discipleship is a team sport. We never see any of the Twelve figuring out how to follow Jesus all on their own. Even Jesus calls Peter, James, and John to accompany him when he goes to pray in the Garden at Gethsemane. "Two are better than one, because they have a good reward for their toil. For if they fall, one will lift up his fellow; but woe to him who is alone when he falls and has not another to lift him up" (Ecclesiastes 4:9-10).

St. Francis de Sales wrote that "in the world those who aim at a devout life require to be united one with another by a holy friendship, which excites, stimulates and encourages them in well-doing."[30] Holy friendship. We need that, don't we? Someone who builds us up. A friend who perseveres through hardship and failure and believes in the vision God has for our lives—especially when we feel lost and forgotten. Holy friendship loves through suffering, speaks truth when it's not easy, and stirs our hearts when we lose motivation to grow in holiness.

Is there someone you turn to when you need advice on something? Do you have a prayer warrior in your life who will go to battle for you at the drop of a hat? Do you have a regular and intentional practice of sharing your life in Christ with someone? Someone you get together with regularly (even sacrificing sleep or other priorities to meet)?

For many Christians, the answer to these questions is no.

Pray about who might be this kind of friend for you. Likely, it'll take sacrifice and perseverance to meet regularly. For this practice, we're not suggesting you seek out a mentor or a spiritual director (though these are helpful people to have in your network too). Your friend is a companion, a fellow disciple of Jesus to walk the journey with. If you are married, try to think of someone *besides your spouse*. Also, for married and unmarried persons alike, men should meet with men, and women with women. Don't travel solo in your Christian life anymore. From now on, strive to follow Jesus with a friend.

See appendix A, "Prayer Partners," for a guide to help you get started with a spiritual friend or prayer partner.

11

Reconciled

He will heal you.

What Does God Want?

When you think about your life, do you ever find yourself wondering "What does God want?" It's natural for Christians to wonder, and it's also natural for the answer to change over time. Two very different ways exist to consider this question: do we consider it as "from me" or "for me"?

- What does God want from me?
- What does God want for me?

God, whose very nature is love, does not want anything *from us* except that which is ultimately best *for us*. And what does God want for us? St. Paul lists fruit of the Spirit as: "Love, joy, peace, patience, kindness, goodness, faithfulness, gentleness, self-control" (Galatians 5:22-23). That's one beautiful list of things our heavenly Father wants for his children!

We've identified "repentance" (*metanoia*) as the recalibration of our hearts toward God—our ongoing consent for God to keep saving and shaping us. Remembering what God wants for us (the fruits of the Spirit) provides a vital context for reflecting on repentance. Turning back to God allows us to receive more of his peace, his love, his joy.

In chapter 3, Broken By Sin, we explored the idea of original sin and the conflict, *the gap*, it creates in our lives and in the world. As we talk more of sin and repentance, we may experience a range of emotional reactions, and this discussion may even bring to mind thoughts about historical and cultural reactions. Perhaps you're thinking of extremes, opposite reactions that cultural groups have taken: an oppressive focus on sin and guilt, or a naïve assumption of innocence. It's the old debate about whether people are basically good or evil.

As we said in Part 1, from a Christian perspective, humans are *both* wonderfully good and dangerously conflicted by sin. Remember that Russian novelist Aleksandr Solzhenitsyn discussing how "the line dividing good and evil cuts through the heart of every human being"? Jesus takes both sides of this line very seriously. His radical, "scandalous mercy" toward the greatest sinners reminds us of our inalienable dignity, and his repeated calls to repentance remind us of our need for him.

Detox

Andrea

A couple years ago, my husband and I joined in on a popular diet trend: not eating any sugar for thirty days. The first few days were fine (whatever, I don't *need* dessert after dinner, right?). The next few days were marked by sugar withdrawal (gosh, I'm tired and cranky). Then there were the dreams (wait, did I eat a donut yesterday? No! I dreamed that!). Finally, after about twenty-five of the thirty days, I started to see the benefits: less hunger between meals, more mental clarity, consistent energy throughout the day, fewer mood swings. It took me twenty-five days to find freedom from something as banal as *sugar*. I had no idea how much power this simple ingredient had over my body, my mood, my mind.

When I had a major moment of *metanoia* a number of years ago, I went to Confession for the first time in ten years. I confessed all that was on my heart. But having done it once, the graces of the sacrament helped me see the remaining sins still enslaving me. Over the course of a few months, I went to Confession multiple times, as I formed my conscience and recognized more sins I didn't even realize I was committing. It was the ultimate detox. As I confessed my sins, I realized with increasing clarity the grip sin and sin-inducing habits had on my life.

In a manner with far more eternal significance than my sugar detox, detoxing from sin gave me ultimate clarity—I saw the freedom God wanted for me. While sin was and is still tempting and attractive, ultimately the false promises of the moral version of a "sugar hit" aren't worth giving up the freedom, life, and truth God's ways offer.

Sin Revisited

In Part 1, we talked about sin in general terms, as *something* that is *not right*; the *something* that causes many of the gaps in our lives, in our world, and in our communion with God. Jesus comes into the gaps, heals those rifts, and invites us to reconciliation.

The Church gives words to a dynamic we're all familiar with: some sins are worse than others. The two degrees of sin defined by the *Catechism* are *mortal* and *venial* sins.

> *Mortal sin* destroys charity in the heart of man by a grave violation of God's law; it turns man away from God, who is his ultimate end and his beatitude, by preferring an inferior good to him. *Venial sin* allows charity to subsist, even though it offends and wounds it. (*Catechism*, 1855)

A mortal sin is like a mortal wound—it endangers our life. Jesus offers us a path to abundant and everlasting life. Consciously going against God by choosing a mortal sin endangers our connection to that life. If we've sinned mortally, we need to again seek God's life through the Sacrament of Reconciliation:

> Mortal sin, by attacking the vital principle within us—that is, charity—necessitates a new initiative of God's mercy and a conversion of heart which is normally accomplished within the setting of the sacrament of reconciliation. (*Catechism*, 1856)

If you are just starting out on the road of discipleship or returning to it after time away, certain sins, for which you may want to seek God's forgiveness, likely jump to mind. Some of the effects of the Sacrament of Reconciliation are graces that help us resist future sin and help us grow in charity. Like with the sugar detox from earlier, it may take some time to discover the graces of giving up sin, but keep asking God to show you the freedom he's offering.

Jesus Overcomes Our Obstacles

Andrea

I have to imagine Peter felt awful on Holy Saturday. Fell asleep in Gethsemane; denied, denied, denied Jesus; and now, his Savior was dead. So many regrets. So much left unsaid. I'm sorry, Lord.

For Peter, and for us, sin was not the end. In the grace of the resurrection, Peter was allowed to renew his love and devotion to the Lord.

When they had finished breakfast, Jesus said to Simon Peter, "Simon, son of John, do you love me more than these?" He said to him, "Yes, Lord; you know that I love you." He said to him, "Feed my lambs." A second time he said to him, "Simon, son of John, do you love me?" He said to him, "Yes, Lord; you know that I love you." He said to him, "Tend my sheep." He said to him the third time, "Simon, son of John, do you love me?" Peter was grieved because he said to him the third time,

"Do you love me?" And he said to him, "Lord, you know everything; you know that I love you." Jesus said to him, "Feed my sheep." (John 21:15-17)

"Reconciliation" gives us a rich, biblical word for God's healing and restoring work. To reconcile is to remove the tension between two parties, to restore a previously fractured bond.

Jesus accomplished reconciliation between the world and God once and for all by his death and resurrection. Yet each of us enters and experiences this reconciliation over time as we cling more fully to him.

God gave the Church a visible means of experiencing his reconciling love. In the Sacrament of Reconciliation, we see, hear, touch, feel, and know, with a blessed assurance, that we are embraced, forgiven, healed, and strengthened by the Lord himself. This truly is good news!

Human weakness and sin create obstacles in our life with Christ, but Jesus can always overcome these blocks if we let him. Like Peter, we need to jump from the boat and swim to the risen Jesus, begging for reconciliation. The Lord knows everything. He knows your heart. Run to him, even when you've failed or sinned or turned away; he will heal you and restore your identity as his disciple.

Why Go to Confession?

Why go to Confession?

While visiting a Roman prison, Pope Benedict gave us a pointed answer to this question. A transcript of his conversation with inmates gives us all a better perspective on this sacrament.

Does his answer add anything to your own understanding?

I would say two things. The first: naturally, if you kneel down and with true love for God pray that God forgives you, he forgives you. It has always been the teaching of the Church that [when] one, with true repentance—that is, not only in order to avoid punishment, difficulty, but for love of the good, for love of God—asks for forgiveness, he is pardoned by God. This is the first part. If I honestly know that I have done evil, and if love for goodness, a desire for goodness, is reborn within me, [and if there is] repentance for not having responded to this love, and I ask forgiveness of God, who is the Good, he gives it to me. But there is a second element: sin is not only a "personal," individual thing between myself and God. Sin always has a social dimension, a horizontal one. With my personal sin, even if perhaps no one knows it, I have damaged the communion of the Church, I have sullied the communion of the Church, and I have sullied humanity. And therefore this social, horizontal dimension of sin requires that it be absolved also at the level of the human community, of the community of the Church, almost physically. Thus this second dimension of sin, which is not only against God but concerns the community too, demands the sacrament, and the sacrament is the great gift in which through confession, we can free ourselves from this thing and we can really receive forgiveness in the sense of a full readmission to the community of the living Church, of the body of Christ. And so, in this sense, the necessary absolution by the priest, the sacrament, is not an imposition—let us say—on the limits of God's goodness, but, on the contrary, it is an expression of the goodness of God because it shows me also concretely, in the communion of the Church, I have received pardon and can start anew. Thus, I would say, hold on to these two dimensions: the vertical one, with God, and the horizontal one, with the community of the Church and humanity.

The absolution of the priest, sacramental absolution, is necessary to really absolve me of this link with evil and to fully reintegrate me into the will of God, into the vision of God, into his Church and to give me sacramental, almost bodily, certitude: God forgives me; he receives me into the community of his children. I think that we must learn how to understand the Sacrament of Penance in this sense: as a possibility of finding again, almost physically, the goodness of the Lord, the certainty of reconciliation.[31]

Falling and Rising

James

I signed up for World Youth Day 2000 to see Rome. I boarded the plane as a tourist, but within hours, I realized I wasn't in for your normal tourist excursion.

Our group planned to walk through the Holy Door of St. Peter's Basilica. Before going, the priest encouraged us to make a good confession. I had not been to Confession in five years! So I went. After I confessed my sins, the priest said he had a few questions. Over the next ten minutes, he asked me question after question, helping me examine my conscience thoroughly. I was sorry for all the things he asked me about, and he gave me a stiff penance . . . two Rosaries!

It was my first adult, mature confession. It should have felt amazing to let all of those sins go, but I felt more ashamed when I left than when I walked in. I moped around hopeless, wondering how I could possibly avoid those sins in the future. The Act of Contrition I had made seemed unattainable. I was distraught.

After a while the priest noticed me and my mood. He asked what was going on. "I don't see the point of Confession if I can't even imagine not committing these same sins again and again! My Act of Contrition was a lie. There's no way I can keep that promise."

"James!" he said. "That's not what Confession is all about. God wants us to live our lives fully and freely and use the gifts he has given us. When we trip and fall, he wants us to run to him and let his love and mercy clean us up and get us moving in the right direction."

That post-Confession confession changed everything for me. I had felt impossible, unfixable, and destined to keep sinning. On that day, Jesus became approachable, a source of never-ending mercy. Of course, I still sin, but God's mercy has become my foundation. I know who to turn to every time I fall.

Practice: Prepare for Confession

Andrea

Like so many of us, I've had the experience of needing to apologize to someone I love. I knew what I had done was wrong, I was honestly really sorry I'd done it at all, and the break in our friendship was killing me. Though I was incredibly nervous to go to my friend and ask for forgiveness, I longed for reconciliation.

As I prepared to apologize, I rehearsed the words in my head over and over. I wanted to name exactly what I'd done so that my loved one would know that I understood why what I had done was harmful. I knew I wanted to ask her for forgiveness and to restore our relationship.

This is the core of the Sacrament of Reconciliation. Recognizing we have done something to harm our relationship with God by breaking that communion he desires for us, we approach the sacrament to name our wrongs, to say we are sorry, and to ask for forgiveness. We ask to start over, to be friends again, to reconcile.

Returning to the Sacrament of Reconciliation can understandably strike fear in many hearts. Reconciliation forces us to be vulnerable—naming our brokenness and inadequacy.

But the beautiful promise of the Sacrament of Reconciliation is that God *longs to forgive you*. There is no need for fear. God entered into our human condition, experienced all the suffering our sin causes, so that he could free us from sin's tyranny. In the words of St. Paul, "We beseech you on behalf of Christ, be reconciled to God. For our sake he made him to be sin who knew no sin, so that in him we might become the righteousness of God" (2 Corinthians 5:20-21). God promises freedom, wholeness, life, righteousness. There is no judgment, only forgiveness.

To prepare to receive the sacrament, it helps to examine your conscience and specifically identify how you've turned away from your relationship with God. Give yourself time to sit in a quiet space, and review the examination of conscience in appendix B, or use some other examination of conscience, to prepare to confess your sins and ask God for forgiveness.

Appendix A

Prayer Partners:
A Guide for Growth in Christ

"As iron sharpens iron, / so one person sharpens another."
—Proverbs 27:17, NIV

"Missionary disciples accompany missionary disciples."
—Pope Francis, *Evangelii Gaudium*, 173

*". . . in the world those who aim at a devout life require
to be united one with another by a holy friendship, which
excites, stimulates and encourages them in well-doing."*
—St. Francis de Sales, *Introduction to the Devout Life*, 203

In Brief

- Meet regularly with a prayer partner—a Christian friend—for the express purpose of sharing your journey of discipleship with one another through conversation, accountability and prayer. Meet at least once a month, ideally twice a month. College students: meet at least twice a month, ideally every week.

- Possible adaptation: this could work in very small groups of three or four. Any number above four is too large for the type of accountability and sharing required.

- Guiding questions: What is the Lord teaching you? How is your prayer life? How can I pray for you?

Tips and Instructions

- Make it comfortable and enjoyable, a treat you look forward to—coffee, breakfast, lunch break, something that will fit in naturally with life. Don't overthink this!

- Bring your Bible, a pen, and a small notebook.

Sample Outline

1. Catch up briefly ("How are you?"). Make sure to transition to the following rather soon.

2. "How has prayer been going?" Share how faithful you have been (or haven't been!) to prayer, and any joys or challenges you're experiencing. Share how the Lord has spoken to you in a prayer time or in your life. If there's a specific verse or passage that stuck with you, open your Bible or notebook and read it, sharing what you think

it means for you. Allow natural conversation to flow from this.

3. If one or both of you are experiencing difficulties (most people do), discuss possible solutions and strategies. Set specific goals to help you be faithful, and inform one another of these goals. See Tips & Troubleshooting for Prayer on the next page for ideas.

4. Talk about how and whom God is calling you to serve/love/care for/reach out to.

5. "How can I pray for you?" Be specific, sharing intentions for yourself rather than others.

6. "Is there anything you want me to bug you about?" In other words, do you need any accountability on something (exercise, diet, a spiritual goal, breaking a bad habit, a specific way to be a better spouse or parent, taking the next step on a good goal in your life, etc.)? If your partner says yes, remember to ask about this in subsequent chats.

7. Close by praying for one another, ideally each praying in his or her own words, voicing the intentions just shared by the other. Keep praying for one another individually between get-togethers, and send little messages here and there (Bible quotes, notes of encouragement, reminders of something for which they requested accountability).

Keep the topic of conversation focused on your lives of prayer and action. Keep it Christ-centered. You'll be tempted to turn towards casual conversation, theoretical matters, or political/religious opining. Some of this is fine and natural, but work very hard to keep it grounded in real, practical discipleship. Jesus is speaking, guiding, stretching, and helping you through your real life. That's where your focus must remain.

Tips & Troubleshooting for Prayer

These tips can help you and your prayer partner's individual prayer.

1. Make an appointment. The same time each day is helpful. The best time is the time that you will do it; however, best practice and the wisdom of the saints recommends first thing in the morning. This way it is a priority, and if something does come up, you can reschedule it for later in the day. "Morning by morning he wakens . . . / my ear / to hear" (Isaiah 50:4).

2. Shoot for at least fifteen minutes a day. If you're already there, add five minutes, until you hit thirty minutes. If you find yourself distracted by the clock, set a timer for your length of time and forget about it until it goes off.

3. Don't overlook the human mechanisms that will enable you to be faithful. Set your clothes out the night before; put it on your calendar; set the coffeemaker the night before so it's ready to go for your morning coffee date with Jesus; put your alarm on the other side of room so you

don't throw away fifteen minutes of your life by hitting snooze two or three times. If you find yourself falling asleep during prayer, sit up at the table, stand, or pace.

4. If you miss a day or two, don't get discouraged. Simply return to your plan and begin again. Try extra hard not to miss two days in a row.

5. If you are distracted, simply persevere. Take those distractions to prayer or write them down so you can return to them at a better time. Keep a crucifix or picture nearby that helps you return your attention to God. Ask your guardian angel to take care of it. God does not mind distractions. He desires the love with which we return our focus to him. Many find it helpful to use a small notebook or journal to help focus their payer times.

6. Do not over idealize your prayer. Most of the time, it won't "feel" perfect or life-changing. There will be unexpected interruptions, dryness, distractions, etc. You will experience seasons of joy and struggle in prayer. After a prayer time, resist the temptation to evaluate how it went. Just be faithful, and over time you will grow in your ability to pray and to follow the subtle promptings of the Spirit throughout your day.

7. If you feel at a loss for what to pray about, don't hesitate to just talk to God about whatever is on your mind. For example, issues at work, tensions in the family, issues with kids, an upcoming trip you are looking forward to,

or thoughts and affections that have been preoccupying you. Or use a simple structure such as the Our Father, or the following three points to guide your prayer: (1) Thank you, (2) I'm sorry, (3) Please.

Appendix B

A Brief Examination of Conscience Based on the Ten Commandments

I am the LORD your God: you shall not have strange Gods before me.
Have I treated people, events, or things as more important than God?

You shall not take the name of the LORD your God in vain.
Have my words, actively or passively, put down God, the Church, or people?

Remember to keep holy the LORD's Day.
Do I go to Mass every Sunday (or Saturday Vigil) and on Holy Days of Obligation (January 1; the Ascension; August 15; November 1; December 8; December 25)? Do I avoid, when possible, work that impedes worship to God, joy for the Lord's

Day, and proper relaxation of mind and body? Do I look for ways to spend time with family or in service on Sunday?

Honor your father and your mother.
Do I show my parents due respect? Do I seek to maintain good communication with my parents where possible? Do I criticize them for lacking skills I think they should have?

You shall not kill.
Have I harmed another through physical, verbal, or emotional means, including gossip or manipulation of any kind?

You shall not commit adultery.
Have I respected the physical and sexual dignity of others and of myself?

You shall not steal.
Have I taken or wasted time or resources that belonged to another?

You shall not bear false witness against your neighbor.
Have I gossiped, told lies, or embellished stories at the expense of another?

You shall not covet your neighbor's spouse.
Have I honored my spouse with my full affection and exclusive love?

You shall not covet your neighbor's goods.
Am I content with my own means and needs, or do I compare myself to others unnecessarily?

Notes

1. This quote is from the *Catechism*, paragraph 1. We will refer to the *Catechism of the Catholic Church* as *Catechism* here, and the numbers following refer to the marked paragraphs of the *Catechism*.

2. For more on this quote and Fr. Ronald Rolheiser, see Ronald Rolheiser, *Prayer: Our Deepest Longing*, (Cincinnati: OH, Franciscan Media, 2013) 37-38.

3. Aleksandr Solzhenitsyn, in Daniel J. Mahoney, *Aleksandr Solzhenitsyn: The Ascent from Ideology* (New York: Rowman & Littlefield Publishers, Inc., 2001), 50. Accessed online Sept 15, 2017, at https://books.google.com/books?id=-zaM0Gp8ZRkC&printsec.

4. Dr. Bob Schuchts has books and materials that further enumerate this presentation of these seven sins. Ave Maria Press publishes some of these materials if you are interested in learning more about his approach.

5. Dr. Bob Schuchts *Be Transformed: The Healing Power of the Sacraments*, "Seven Deadly Wounds" (Notre Dame, IN: Ave Maria Press, 2017), 30.

6. Vatican II, *Gaudium et Spes*, 22, http://www.vatican.va/archive/hist_councils/ii_vatican_council/documents/vat-ii_const_19651207_gaudium-et-spes_en.html.

7. Pope St. John Paul II, *Redemptoris Missio*, 55, referencing Letter to the Fifth Plenary Assembly of Asian Bishops' Conferences (June 23, 1990), 4: *L'Osservatore Romano*, July 18, 1990, http://w2.vatican.va/content/john-paul-ii/en/encyclicals/documents/hf_jp-ii_enc_07121990_redemptoris-missio.html#%242S.

8. St. Athanasius, quoted in the *Catechism*, 460.

9. Walter Lewis, *The Grand Miracle: And Other Selected Essays on Theology and Ethics from God* (New York: Random House Publishing Group, 1970), 85.

10. St. Augustine, *Confessions* (New York: Oxford University Press, 1991), 3.

11. *General Directory for Catechesis*, 55, http://www.vatican.va/roman_curia/congregations/cclergy/documents/rc_con_ccatheduc_doc_17041998_directory-for-catechesis_en.html.

12. Ibid., 56.

13. Joseph Cardinal Ratzinger, *Introduction to Christianity* (San Francisco, CA: Ignatius Press), 81.

14. Recall that in chapter 1, on page 18, "In a Nutshell," we pointed to the opening paragraph of the *Catechism* as a potent summary of the good news. You may wish to review this page again, having now reflected on the entire contents of this chapter.

15. C. S. Lewis, *Mere Christianity* (New York, NY: HarperCollins Publishers, 2001), 206.

16. Pope Benedict XVI, Inaugural Homily, April 24, 2005, https://w2.vatican.va/content/benedict-xvi/en/homilies/2005/documents/hf_ben-xvi_hom_20050424_inizio-pontificato.html.

17. Adapted by The Evangelical Catholic with permission from "The Wheel Illustration," copyright 1976 by the Navigators.

18. St. Teresa of Avila, *The Collected Works of St. Teresa of Avila*, translated by Kieran Kavanaugh, OCD, and Otilio Rodriguez, OCD (Washington, DC: ICS Publications, 1987), 44.

19. St. John of the Cross, "The Sayings of Light and Love," no. 100, in *The Collected Works of St. John of the Cross*, translated by Kieran Kavanaugh, OCD, and Otilio Rodrigues, OCD (Washington DC: ICS Publications, 1991), 92.

20. Here we'll reflect specifically on the elements of the Liturgy of the Eucharist, the part of the Mass that starts after the readings, when the bread and wine are brought forward to the altar. We'll dive further into the role of Scripture in the life of a disciple in Part 3.

21. Pope Benedict XVI, *Sacramentum Caritatis*, February 22, 2007, 83, 84, http://w2.vatican.va/content/benedict-xvi/en/apost_exhortations/documents/hf_ben-xvi_exh_20070222_sacramentum-caritatis.html..

22. St. Gregory the Great, *Ep. 4, 31*, quoted in Garcia M. Columbas, *Reading God: Lectio Divina* (Winona, IN: BMH Publications, 1993), 42-44, emphasis added.

23. Pope Benedict XVI, Address of His Holiness Benedict XVI to the Participants in the International Congress Organized to Commemorate the 40th Anniversary of the Dogmatic Constitution on Divine Revelation "Dei Verbum," September 16, 2005, http://w2.vatican.va/content/benedict-xvi/en/speeches/2005/september/documents/hf_ben-xvi_spe_20050916_40-dei-verbum.html.

24. Of course, no human parents are perfect, but God is. Understanding God as "Father" does not mean God is male, nor that God lacks what we understand as feminine characteristics. God "is neither man nor woman," and "the respective 'perfections' of man and woman reflect something of the infinite perfection of God: those of a mother and those of a father" (*Catechism*, 370, referencing cf. Isaiah 49:14-15; 66:13; Psalm 131:2-3; Hosea 11:1-4; Jeremiah 3:4-19).

25. Jean Vanier, *Jesus, the Gift of Love* (New York: The Crossroad Publishing Company, 1994), 47.

26. Henri J. M. Nouwen, *Out of Solitude: Three Meditations on the Christian Life* (Notre Dame, IN: Ave Maria Press, 1974), 40.

27. *Catechism of the Catholic Church*, 537.

28. "She is clearly the mother of the members of Christ . . . since she has by her charity joined in bringing about the birth of believers in the Church, who are members of its head." *Catechism of the Catholic Church*, 963.

29. *Catechism of the Catholic Church*, 501, referencing *Lumen Gentium*, 63; cf. John 19:26-27; Romans 8:29; Revelation 12:17.

30. St. Francis of Sales, *Introduction to the Devout Life*, 203, accessed October 10, 2017, at http://www.ccel.org/ccel/desales/devout_life.

31. Pope Benedict XVI, Responses of His Holiness Benedict XVI to the Questions Posed by the Inmates, December 18, 2011, accessed at http://w2.vatican.va/content/benedict-xvi/en/speeches/2011/december/documents/hf_ben-xvi_spe_20111218_rebibbia-risposte.html.

About the Authors

Andrea Jackson studied English Language and Literature as an undergraduate at Harvard University and earned a master's degree in Divinity from the Boston College School of Theology and Ministry. She started intentionally following Jesus as a sophomore in college when another student showed her which next steps to take in her life of discipleship. Andrea worked as a pastoral associate at a parish in the Archdiocese of Boston for four years before joining the team of The Evangelical Catholic as a writer and ministry consultant in 2018. She lives with her husband in Milwaukee, Wisconsin.

Andre Lesperance is a senior ministry consultant and writer at The Evangelical Catholic. He has worked in full-time Catholic ministry and education since 2003 and holds a master's degree in theology from Marquette University. In both his personal and professional life, Andre's passion lies in helping others to grow in the riches of life in Christ Jesus by identifying and taking their next steps. He lives with his wife and four children near Milwaukee, Wisconsin.

the WORD among us®
The *Spirit* of Catholic Living

This book was published by The Word Among Us. Since 1981, The Word Among Us has been answering the call of the Second Vatican Council to help Catholic laypeople encounter Christ in the Scriptures.

The name of our company comes from the prologue to the Gospel of John and reflects the vision and purpose of all of our publications: to be an instrument of the Spirit, whose desire is to manifest Jesus' presence in and to the children of God. In this way, we hope to contribute to the Church's ongoing mission of proclaiming the gospel to the world so that all people would know the love and mercy of our Lord and grow more deeply in their faith as missionary disciples.

Our monthly devotional magazine, *The Word Among Us*, features meditations on the daily and Sunday Mass readings and currently reaches more than one million Catholics in North America and another half-million Catholics in one hundred countries around the world. Our book division, The Word Among Us Press, publishes numerous books, Bible studies, and pamphlets that help Catholics grow in their faith.

To learn more about who we are and what we publish, visit us at www.wau.org. There you will find a variety of Catholic resources that will help you grow in your faith.

Embrace His Word, Listen to God . . .

www.wau.org